MEXICAN MICROWAVE COOKERY

A Collection of Mexican Recipes
Using the Microwave Oven

by
Carol Medina Maze

FISHER BOOKS

Publishers: Howard W. Fisher
Helen V. Fisher
Fred W. Fisher

Coordinator: Helen V. Fisher
Editor: Retha M. Davis
Art Director: Josh Young
Drawings: David Fischer

Published by Fisher Books
3499 N. Campbell Avenue, Suite 909
Tucson, Arizona 85719
(602) 325-5263

Cover photos courtesy PACE® Picante Sauce.

**Library of Congress
Cataloging-in-Publication Data**
Maze, Carol Medina
Mexican microwave cookery
Includes index
1. Cookery, Mexican. 2. Microwave cookery. I. Title.
TX716.M4M39 1988
ISBN 1-55561-007-2

Printed in U.S.A.
Printing 10 9 8 7 6 5 4 3 2

Notice: The information in this book is true and complete to the best of our knowledge. It is offered with no guarantees on the part of the author or Fisher Books. Author and publisher disclaim all liability in connection with the use of this book.

CONTENTS

Dedication

To my husband Richard
and children Lucas and Cassandra:
Thanks for the encouragement.

Biography

Carol Medina Maze is a native of the Southwest, having grown up in Las Cruces, New Mexico. She has developed over 140 authentic, traditional recipes for the microwave oven. Many have been handed down through her family. Carol has blended her appreciation of native Mexican food with her professional training as a home economics teacher in developing and testing these recipes. She received her degree in home economics from New Mexico State University and resides in Phoenix, Arizona.

Acknowledgments

I thank my mother, Mary Louise Medina, for her invaluable contributions of traditional recipes. Some of these recipes are renditions of my great-aunt's recipes. My great-aunt, Guadalupe Medina, established her culinary reputation cooking for ranches and inns in Southern New Mexico during the early 1900s.

My father, Robert Medina, published the first edition of this book through Bilingue Publications and reviewed my Spanish usage in the manuscripts. My husband, Richard, was the primary support in the development of the text. A final note of thanks goes to Virginia Lark who typed and edited the first edition text.

PREFACE

This cookbook was written for those who enjoy Mexican foods. Traditionally, Mexican foods took time to prepare and required the use of many pots and pans, as well as various burners and the oven. With today's fast pace of living, one may not find time to spend in the kitchen on a particular meal. This book gives you a way to prepare Mexican dishes in about one-third the time. You save time, energy and effort, with fewer dishes and less cleanup. And you get all this without sacrificing nutrition, appearance or flavor. Recipes in this book are based on authentic and traditional Mexican recipes, but written specifically for microwave cooking.

When I purchased my microwave oven, I made it a point to do more than just heat water in it. I have always enjoyed preparing Mexican food, but I could not find very many Mexican recipes for the microwave oven. Coincidentally, my father was publishing an Hispanic literature newsletter and wanted to include some Mexican recipes. This gave me an opportunity to develop some of our family recipes for the microwave which met with my father's encouragement.

As I researched the Southwestern Mexican cuisine, I found many of the traditional recipes could be adapted to the microwave oven. As time went on, it became desirable to compile the recipes in a single cookbook, *Mexican Microwave Cookery*. I have now revised and added more recipes which I present in this book.

My culinary experience is based on my family life in the Mesilla Valley of New Mexico and on my training as a home economist. I became a 7th- and 8th-grade home-economics teacher where I learned the art of teaching others the nuances of food preparation. Since the publication of my first Mexican cookbook, I have presented cooking demonstrations before live audiences and on local and syndicated cable TV. My recipes have been reviewed in syndicated newspaper columns. My working life has taken me to Northern New Mexico and Arizona where I learned a great deal about local customs involving Mexican cooking. My sister, Agatha Rodriguez, has lived in San Antonio, Odessa and El Paso, Texas. She has shared much of her knowledge about "Tex-Mex" cooking with me over the years. I believe this has been useful in writing recipes that hopefully are understandable to you.

¡Salud y Buen Apetito!
To your health and good eating!

INTRODUCTION TO MEXICAN COOKERY

In recent years, Mexican foods have become increasingly popular. These foods are colorful and have very distinct flavors and aromas brought about by the chiles and spices contained in them. Fresh or dried spices, such as oregano, whole cominos (cumin), azafrán (wild saffron), fresh garlic, fresh or dried cilantro (coriander), fresh onion, fresh bell pepper, chiles, tomatoes and tomatillos constitute those "special secret ingredients" which bring out the flavor.

Traditionally, Mexican foods are cooked slowly to enhance the characteristic flavors. In microwave cooking, the flavors and aromas of the chiles and spices are equally good. Recipes in this book have been developed and tested through use of the microwave oven. These recipes are categorized into various dishes or "comidas." For example, dishes which contain corn or flour are referred to as "comidas de masa." Foods containing chicken are referred to as "comidas de pollo."

Recipes provide information on required power levels, cooking time and number of servings as well as the ingredient list and method of preparation.

The Microwave Oven

The microwave oven has become an integral part of the kitchen in many homes. It is convenient and saves time.

Once the microwave oven is turned on, microwaves are emitted. Microwaves pass through non-metallic materials, such as glass, ceramic, paper and plastics, penetrating and cooking food.

Microwaves are reflected by metal materials and will not cook food contained in metal dishes. You must be sure to use the appropriate microwave cookware.

Microwaves cook from the outside toward the center, therefore many foods may need to be stirred during the cooking time. Rotating dishes during cooking will also help ensure uniform cooking.

Various makes and models of microwave ovens on today's market have different heat and time settings. The heat settings are the power levels which regulate the microwave energy needed to cook a particular food. Time settings simply control the length of cooking time for a given heat setting.

In preparing my recipes, I used percent power. For your convenience, I prepared the following chart for you to use with your particular microwave oven. Some microwave ovens do not have variable heat settings. They cook only at 100% power; heat is controlled only by the length of cooking time.

The following table shows equivalent heat settings for different makes and models of most microwave ovens. For example, if a recipe calls for 70% power, that is equivalent to a heat-select setting of 7, a cooking level of medium-high power, a fractional power level of 2/3, and a temperature level of roast. Heat created from microwave energy continues to cook foods after microwaves have penetrated them. Some of the recipes in this book call for a "standing time." This is the period during which heat from the food itself continues to cook food at the end of the actual microwave cooking time.

Some microwave ovens have variable time settings, but cook on high power only. If your microwave oven is of this type, it will be necessary to adjust cooking times for power settings presented in recipes in this book. For example, a dish cooked with a power level of 50% (medium) 20 minutes would be cooked on 100% (high) 10 minutes.

Equivalent Settings

Percent Power	Heat	Cooking Level	Power Level	Temperature
100	10	high	full	high
90	9			sauté
80	8			bake/reheat
70	7	med-hi	2/3	roast
60	6			simmer
50	5	medium	1/2	defrost high
40	4			defrost low
30	3	med-low	1/3	soften
20	2			warm
10	1	low	1/10	low
0		rest		

Microwave Cookware

There is a variety of cookware on the market that is safe to use in microwave ovens. The following dishes are recommended for preparing recipes in this book: casserole dishes (1-1/2-quart, 2-quart, 2-1/2-quart, 3-quart, and for candy recipes, 5-quart); flat-bottom casserole dishes (8-inches-square or 12" x 8"); glass measuring cups (2-cup and 2-quart); microwave browning dish; glass pie plate and glass loaf pan (8" x 4" x 2").

The microwave browning dish has a special coating on the bottom. When the dish is preheated, it will actually brown foods such as tortillas and fajitas. Be aware that other flat-bottom dishes are not designed for browning foods in the microwave oven. Although I recommend preheating a browning dish 4 to 5 minutes, follow the manufacturer's directions for preheating your dish so as not to damage it or compromise safety.

Caution: Be sure to use hot pads or oven mitts when handling a preheated browning dish.

A new cookware product, which I found to be of great value for preparing stews, beans and meat recipes, is the microwave pressure cooker. Several microwave pressure cooker recipes are included in this book. If using a pressure cooker, be sure to review your manufacturer's directions before use.

Warning: Do not use a regular pressure cooker that is designed for stove-top cooking. When removing a microwave pressure cooker from your microwave, be sure to use oven mitts or hot pads to protect your hands. The pressure cooker will get hot!

Some recipes call for a microwave-safe ring mold. If you do not have one, you can create one by inverting a custard cup in the center of a round, glass cake dish or shallow casserole. The ring shape allows for more even cooking for such things as meat loaf.

If you plan to make a lot of microwave candy, you may want to invest in a microwave-safe candy thermometer. Don't try to use your regular candy thermometer, meat thermometer or oven thermometer. They will not work in the microwave. Stores specializing in microwave ovens and accessories or major department stores should have microwave-safe candy thermometers available.

Tips & Facts on Microwave Cooking

Recipes in this book require various types of coverings for the cooking dish. If a recipe states to microwave without mention of covering the dish, the dish should be *uncovered* during cooking. If the recipe states to "cover with waxed paper," then use a piece of waxed paper *large enough to cover the dish completely* before cooking. The same applies for recipes calling for lids or a plastic-wrap covering. If the recipe simply states to "cover and microwave," a microwave-safe lid, waxed paper, plastic wrap or a paper towel can be used.

Both density and moisture content of the food may make a difference in overall cooking time. As a rule of thumb, moist foods cook faster. Foods with a thicker consistency or greater mass take longer to cook.

Placing a casserole on top of an inverted bowl will allow microwaves to penetrate evenly around the dish. Stirring, rearranging foods and rotating dishes also results in more even cooking.

Microwave energy may be weakened or may suddenly surge because of a change in household current. For this reason, cooking times may not always be precise and may have to be increased or decreased to compensate.

Different microwave ovens require different cooking times due to atmospheric conditions, elevation and electric power. *It is important to know the wattage of your microwave oven.* Recipes in this book were prepared in a 650-watt oven. If your oven operates at a different wattage, you may need to adjust cooking times accordingly.

To compensate for variance in atmospheric conditions, elevation and electric power, a test can be done. Measure 1 cup tepid water from the faucet at 78F (25C). Heat the water on 100% (high) until bubbles begin to break. Record the time it takes for this to happen. Recipes in this book were tested in a microwave oven that boiled 1 cup of 78F (25C) water on the average in 2 minutes and 46 seconds at 1300' elevation. Adjusting the cooking time is thus suggested for recipes in this book should you find variance from my test results.

Ingredients & Substitutions

Ingredients called for in these recipes are readily available at most supermarkets. If a particular ingredient is not available, a substitution may have to be used. Following is a list of ingredients and some substitutions that can be used:

Anise seeds: Substitute liquid anise or a licorice flavoring.

Azafrán (wild saffron): Use a very small quantity of turmeric to achieve the yellow color; however, the unique taste of azafrán cannot be achieved with turmeric.

Chiles (fresh green chile): Use canned green chiles.

Cilantro or fresh coriander: Sometimes this herb is referred to as Chinese parsley. There really is no substitute for it except perhaps dried coriander leaves. Use an equivalent quantity called for in recipe.

Cilantro seeds (coriander seeds): Although there is no perfect substitute for coriander seeds, powdered coriander can be used. The flavor of coriander seeds is entirely different from the flavor of fresh coriander leaves.

Cominos, whole (cumin): Use powdered cumin in same quantity as given in recipe.

Masa harina: This is the corn flour primarily used to make corn tortillas. Cornmeal is not a substitute for masa harina.

Mexican chocolate: For 1 ounce of Mexican chocolate, use a combination of 1 (1-oz.) square semisweet chocolate, 2 teaspoons sugar, 1/8 teaspoon vanilla extract and 1/8 teaspoon ground cinnamon.

Oregano (fresh or dried): Use powdered oregano in same quantity as given in recipe.

Perejil (parsley): Use dried parsley in the same quantity given in recipe.

Piloncillo (Mexican brown sugar): Piloncillo is also sold under the name "Panocha." It is sold in a cone shape. Dark-brown sugar can be substituted in the same quantity.

Red chile powder: Use pure ground red chile powder. If the pure powder is not available, other chile powder can be substituted. However, keep in mind that other spices have been added, such as cumin, oregano, salt and garlic.

Tomatillos: These are similar to small green

tomatoes with paper-like husks. If unavailable fresh, you may find them canned and referred to as "tomatillo entero" or "tomate verde." Small green tomatoes, the garden variety, can be substituted though the flavor will not be equivalent.

Vegetable shortening: Traditional Mexican cooking uses lard or bacon drippings. They give foods the authentic traditional taste. Vegetable shortening can be substituted for lard, as specified in recipes. Although shortening has essentially equivalent calories, it works equally well and gives a lighter taste, without saturated animal fats and cholesterol. Vegetable oil is listed as an ingredient in recipes where its liquid properties are preferred to melting lard or vegetable shortening. Conversely, lard or vegetable shortening is used in recipes where its solid texture is desirable. Vegetable oil can be used as a substitute for lard or vegetable shortening, but due to its liquid properties it may be necessary to adjust dry ingredients, such as flour or masa harina.

Hints

To get more juice from citrus fruits, such as oranges, lemons or limes, microwave on 100% (high) 30 seconds before squeezing fruit.

To soften raisins, combine 1 cup raisins with 1/2 cup water. Cover and microwave on 100% (high) 3 to 4 minutes or until raisins are plump and soft.

CHILES y SALSAS

The Rio Grande River Valley of Southern New Mexico is known as the Mesilla Valley. The farmlands of this valley are ideal for growing the long, broad green chile known throughout the Southwest. The rich irrigated fields and the cool night air that flows into the valley from the nearby San Andreas and Organ Mountains make for ideal growing conditions. Come mid-July, people from Las Cruces go to the farms to pick and buy their fresh green chiles. I remember that every summer my mother would bring home a burlap bag of chiles which I was delegated to assist in roasting.

I can recall the aroma of freshly roasted green chiles that would fill the air in the late summer months in Las Cruces. My mother and the neighbors would roast the chiles either in their kitchens, using a cast-iron skillet, or outside on their barbecue grills, if large quantities were being roasted. This practice evolved from the method used by my great grandmother at the turn of the century. In that time, a pit was dug and filled with mesquite wood. The chiles were then roasted on a grill over the glowing mesquite charcoal. This later became a practice of roasting chiles on a wood stove during my grandmother's time. From pit to wood stove to barbecue grill, the transition has accelerated the cooking technique but the tradition of chile and its flavor has more or less remained the same.

I have developed a way to roast the chile faster and without all the work without compromising on the flavor. The microwave oven is used instead of the cast-iron skillet. I roast chiles in the microwave, place them in plastic freezer bags and freeze for later use. Come mid-winter, I simply get a bag of chiles from the freezer, thaw them and prepare them for whatever recipe I am using.

The season of the red chile in the Mesilla Valley is as culturally significant as football and "Diez y Seis de Septiembre," the 16th of September. From mid-September to the first frost, the chile fields transform from green to brilliant red. It was, and still is, a common practice for people to pick and string mature red chiles by the stems into "ristras de chile." You can drive the rural roads of the valley and see the huge strings of vivid red chiles hanging from the porch rafters and walls of the adobe houses. The chiles would also be picked to sun dry in the farmyards and on roof tops. The landscape would be dotted with brilliant red patches of drying chiles in an autumn scene.

When I was four or five, my mother would send me to my great-aunt Lupe to help her in her neighborhood variety store. She would prepare the family chile in a "cedazo" or cone-shaped colander, which at the time seemed very big. She would mash the sof-tened chile pods with a red-chile-stained wooden pestle. The red pulp would ooze through the colander and collect in a big blue enamel pot. She would warn me that chile burns and would display her reddened hands. She would then wash her hands with mild soap and warm water and rinse them in a bowl of white vinegar to relieve the burning.

Lupe would then make the best Chile Colorado from the processed red chile pulp. My preparation of Chile Colorado is a varia-tion of my great-aunt Lupe's recipe. A blender takes the place of the colander, but the flavoring is the same as what she used.

Caution: Chiles can irritate your hands and eyes, particularly if the chile is "hot!" I recommend that you wear rubber gloves when roasting, peeling and scraping chiles. Avoid touching any facial area when han-dling chiles. After handling chiles, wash your hands thoroughly with soap and water.

Preparing Green Chiles

The fresh chiles recommended for these recipes should be either the Anaheim chile, referred to as the California or long green variety, or the New Mexico "chile de ristra" ancho chile, a full broad variety. Use canned chiles, whole or diced, if fresh chiles cannot be found. Fresh green chiles can be prepared by this microwave method or a conventional oven-roasting method.

Power level: medium-high
Cooking time: 14 minutes
Servings: 6 chiles

6 fresh green chiles
Vegetable oil

Rub each chile pod with oil; pierce each pod on both sides with a knife so steam will vent. Place chiles in a flat-bottom casserole. Cover with waxed paper; microwave on 70% (medium-high) 7 minutes. Turn each chile over; rotate dish. Cover and microwave on 70% (medium-high) 7 more minutes. Chiles will not brown or blister. Wrap chiles in a damp cloth; let stand to cool. This helps to separate the skin from the flesh. Remove pods from damp cloth; peel under cool running tap water. Avoid touching your eyes and mouth. You may want to wear rubber gloves when handling chiles.

Conventional Oven-Roasted Method

If your hands are sensitive, wear rubber gloves when handling chile peppers.

12 fresh green chiles

Pierce each pod on both sides with a knife so steam will vent. Line a baking sheet with foil. Place chiles on lined baking sheet; place under broiler unit of a conventional oven, about 5 inches below broiler. Broil pods, turning pods over about every 5 minutes using tongs, until chiles are blistered on all sides. Using a damp cloth, press chile pods to release trapped steam. Wrap pods in damp cloth; cool and peel as above. Avoid touching your eyes and mouth.

Stewed Tomatoes

Power level: high
Cooking time: 5 minutes
Servings: 2 cups

4 medium tomatoes
1/4 cup water

Remove core of tomatoes; cut tomatoes into quarters. Place tomatoes in a 2-quart casserole; add water. Cover and microwave on 100% (high) 5 minutes, rearranging tomatoes after 3 minutes. Remove tomato skins when cool.

Blanched Tomatoes

Power level: high
Cooking time: 2 to 4 minutes
Servings: 2 cups

4 medium tomatoes

Place 4 tomatoes in a 2-quart casserole. Cover and microwave on 100% (high) 2 to 4 minutes, rearranging tomatoes after 2 minutes. Let stand 2 minutes before peeling tomatoes.

Blanched Tomatillos

For authentic flavor in green sauces, use tomatillos.

Power level: high
Cooking time: 4 minutes
Servings: about 1 cup

8 tomatillos

Remove husks, the outer paper-like skins. Cut each tomatillo in half; place in a glass dish. Cover with waxed paper; microwave on 100% (high) 4 minutes, rearranging tomatillos after 2 minutes. Remove skin from tomatillos; chop remaining pulp. If removing skin is difficult, scrape pulp from skin with a spoon.

Tip

Literally translated, tomatillo means "little tomato." Although a tomatillo is a fruit, as are all tomatoes, it is treated as a vegetable. The husk of a tomatillo turns from green to tan as it ripens. Use the tomatillo while the husk is green because once the husk turns tan, the tomatillo may be overripe. When purchasing tomatillos, pick the ones that are enclosed by the husk.

Mexican-Style Stewed Tomatoes

A fresh side dish that complements any meat or seafood entree.

Power level: high
Cooking time: 8 minutes
Servings: 2-1/2 cups

2 tablespoons vegetable oil
2 tablespoons finely chopped onion
2 tablespoons finely chopped bell pepper
1 garlic clove, chopped

1/2 teaspoon dried leaf oregano, crushed
1/2 teaspoon salt
4 medium tomatoes

Place all ingredients except tomatoes in a 2-quart casserole. Cover and microwave on 100% (high) 3 minutes or until vegetables are tender. Remove tomato cores; cut tomatoes in quarters. Add tomatoes to cooked vegetables. Cover and microwave on 100% (high) 5 minutes, stirring vegetables after 3 minutes. When cool, remove skins from tomatoes, if desired.

Microwave Jalapeño Chiles

Jalapeño chiles are very hot! Six pods will go a long way.

Power level: medium-high
Cooking time: 5 minutes
Servings: 6 to 8 jalapeños

6 to 8 fresh jalapeños
Vegetable oil

Rub each jalapeño with oil. Avoid touching eyes or mouth. Place pods in a casserole dish; cover with waxed paper. Microwave on 70% (medium-high) 5 minutes, turning pods over after 2-1/2 minutes. Wrap pods in a damp cloth; let stand to cool. Remove pods from damp cloth; peel under cool running tap water. Slice pods open; remove seeds and membrane. Chop pods, if desired.

Taco Seasoning Mix

Use this mix instead of a 1-1/4-ounce package of commercial taco seasoning mix.

Servings: 3 tablespoons

1 tablespoon red chile powder	1 teaspoon paprika
1/2 teaspoon salt	1 teaspoon cumin powder
1 teaspoon garlic powder	1 teaspoon ground oregano
2 teaspoons onion powder	1 teaspoon sugar

Combine all ingredients in a small bowl until well blended. Store in an airtight container for future use.

Taco Sauce

Everyone's favorite sauce with tacos or other Mexican specialties.

Servings: 1 cup

1 cup chopped green chiles or 1 (7-oz.) can diced green chiles	1 garlic clove, mashed
2 large tomatoes, blanched, page 4, or 1 (8-oz.) can stewed tomatoes	1/4 teaspoon dried leaf oregano
	salt to taste

Chop blanched tomatoes and combine all ingredients until well blended. Place in an airtight container. Refrigerate sauce up to 7 days.

My favorite condiment for Mexican main dishes is this spicy seasoning mix, above. I make my seasoning mix in quadruple amounts so that I can store some of it for later use. The recipe includes paprika which gives a rustic color when the seasoning mix is added to a dish that is microwave-cooked.

Chile Colorado

Red Chile

An excellent chile sauce for tamales, chile meat and other dishes.

Power level: medium-high
Cooking time: 20 minutes
Servings: 3-1/2 cups

20 dried red chile pods, stems and seeds
    removed
1/4 teaspoon cilantro seeds
1/4 teaspoon whole cominos
1 teaspoon dried leaf oregano

1 garlic clove, cut in half
1/4 cup coarsely chopped onion
1 teaspoon salt
3 cups warm water

Place all ingredients in a blender; process until pureed. Place mixture in a 2-quart casserole. Cover and microwave on 70% (medium-high) 20 minutes, stirring after 10 minutes.

Tip

Some recipes in this book use Chile Colorado uncooked. This means that it is not necessary
to cook the pureed mixture before adding to the other recipe.

If dried red-chile pods are unavailable, substitute 1/2 cup pure red-chile powder and
1 tablespoon all-purpose flour. Place chile powder, flour and all remaining ingredients in
a blender; process until smooth. Cook as above.

Salsa Ranchera

Ranch-Style Sauce

Try Salsa Ranchera on eggs or other Mexican dishes.

Power level: high, medium
Cooking time: 8 minutes
Servings: about 3-1/2 cups

2 cups chopped green chiles or 2 (7-oz.)
   cans diced green chiles
2 cups Blanched Tomatoes, page 4, or
   1 (16-oz.) can stewed tomatoes
1 cup chopped onion

1 garlic clove, chopped
1 teaspoon dried leaf oregano, crushed
1/2 teaspoon salt
1/4 teaspoon whole cominos, crushed
1/4 teaspoon cilantro seeds, crushed

Combine all ingredients in a glass bowl. Cover with waxed paper; microwave on 100% (high) 3 minutes or until mixture begins to boil. Reduce microwave setting to 50% (medium); continue cooking 5 minutes. Serve sauce hot or cold. Refrigerate up to 7 days or freeze until ready to use.

Tip

A *molcajete*, pronounced mohl-kah-heh-teh, and *tejolete*, pronounced te-ho-leh-teh, is a three-legged mortar and pestle made of volcanic rock. It is used for grinding spices and making chile sauces. The use of this device can save time, although it is not absolutely required for grinding and mashing. In many of my recipes. I use the term "crushed" for the ingredients cilantro and comino seeds. Crushed cilantro or comino seeds can be made by grinding the seeds in the molcajete. Seeds can also be crushed by using a fork, although they are ground to a finer texture in the molcajete.

Salsa Para Enchiladas Verdes

Sauce for Green-Chile Enchiladas

An excellent sauce for green-chile tamales as well as enchiladas.

Power level: high, medium-high
Cooking time: 7 minutes
Servings: 2 cups

1 tablespoon vegetable oil	2 tablespoons all-purpose flour
1 garlic clove, mashed	1/2 teaspoon ground cominos
1 cup chopped green chiles or 1 (7-oz.) can diced green chiles	1/2 teaspoon salt
	1 cup water

Combine oil and garlic in a 1-1/2-quart casserole. Cover with waxed paper; microwave on 100% (high) 2 minutes. Stir in remaining ingredients. Cover with waxed paper; microwave on 70% (medium-high) 5 minutes. Cool before serving.

Salsa de Jalapeño

Jalapeño Sauce

If you enjoy hot chiles, this salsa is for you.

Power level: high
Cooking time: 2 minutes
Servings: about 2 cups

1 tablespoon vegetable oil
1/4 cup chopped onion
1 garlic clove, chopped
2 cups Blanched Tomatoes, page 4, or 1
   (16-oz) can stewed tomatoes

1 teaspoon dried leaf oregano, crushed
1/2 teaspoon salt
1/4 cup chopped jalapeño chiles or
   1 (4-oz.) can jalapeño chiles

Combine oil, onion and garlic in a 1-1/2-quart casserole. Cover with waxed paper; microwave on 100% (high) 2 minutes. Stir in remaining ingredients. Refrigerate salsa until ready to use.

Salsa de Tomatillo

Green-Tomato Sauce

Serve this colorful sauce on tacos and flautas.

Power level: high
Cooking time: 2 minutes
Servings: about 1-1/2 cups

1 tablespoon lard or vegetable shortening
1/4 cup chopped onion
1/2 teaspoon cilantro seeds, crushed
1 garlic clove, mashed

1 lb. fresh tomatillos, blanched, page 5
1/4 cup chopped green chiles or 1 (4-oz.)
** can diced green chiles**
Salt

Combine lard or shortening, onion, cilantro and garlic in a 1-1/2-quart casserole. Cover with waxed paper; microwave on 100% (high) 2 minutes. Stir in tomatillos and chiles. Add salt to taste. Refrigerate until ready to serve.

Chile Barbecue Sauce

Top any meat or poultry dish with this spicy barbecue sauce.

Power level: medium-high
Cooking time: 20 minutes
Servings: 1 cup

3 tablespoons Taco Seasoning Mix, page
    7, or 1 (1-1/4-oz.) pkg. taco seasoning
    mix
1 tablespoon red chile powder
1/4 cup tomato paste
1 tablespoon Worcestershire sauce

2 tablespoons brown sugar
1 teaspoon dry mustard
2 tablespoons vinegar
1 tablespoon vegetable oil
1 cup water

Combine all ingredients in a glass bowl. Cover with waxed paper; microwave on 70% (medium-high) 20 minutes, stirring after 10 minutes. Refrigerate until ready to use.

Mole Colorado

Red Chile Sauce

The unusual combination of red chile, chocolate, cinnamon and peanut butter gives this Mexican sauce a unique taste. This is the famous sauce used for chicken mole.

Power level: medium-high
Cooking time: 30 minutes
Servings: about 3-1/2 cups

3 cups chicken broth or beef broth
1 (8-oz.) can tomato sauce
3 tablespoons Taco Seasoning Mix, page 7, or 1 (1-1/4-oz.) pkg. taco seasoning mix

2 tablespoons red chile powder
1/3 cup creamy peanut butter
3 (1-oz.) squares semisweet chocolate
2 tablespoons sugar
3/4 teaspoon ground cinnamon

Combine all ingredients in a 2-1/2-quart bowl. Cover with waxed paper; microwave on 70% (medium-high) 30 minutes, stirring every 10 minutes. Refrigerate until ready to use.

Mole Verde

Green Chile Sauce

Another delicious sauce for seasoning chicken or pork.

Power level: medium-high
Cooking time: 30 minutes
Servings: about 4-1/2 cups

1 lb. tomatillos, blanched, unpeeled, page 5
5 jalapeño chiles, page 6, or 1 (4-oz.) can jalapeño chiles
2-1/2 cups chicken broth or beef broth
1 cup coarsely chopped onion
1/4 teaspoon coriander seeds

1/4 cup fresh coriander or parsley
1 garlic clove
1/4 teaspoon whole cominos
1/2 cup chopped walnuts
3/4 cup chopped almonds
1 teaspoon salt
1 tablespoon vegetable oil

Cut blanched tomatillos in half. Place all ingredients in a blender or food processor; process until pureed. Pour sauce in a 2-1/2-quart bowl. Cover with waxed paper; microwave on 70% (medium-high) 30 minutes, stirring after 15 minutes. Refrigerate until ready to use or freeze up to 2 months for later use.

Mole has its origin from the early Aztecs. Mole is a sauce made with chile, nuts, tomatoes or tomatillos and spices. Many moles are prepared with chocolate and cinnamon. Mole can be used as a sauce for turkey, chicken or shredded pork.

Chile con Queso

Chile with Cheese

A creamy chile-cheese sauce, great for dipping tortilla chips.

Power level: high, medium
Cooking time: 9 minutes
Servings: 2-1/2 cups

2 tablespoons vegetable oil
1/2 cup finely chopped onion
1 garlic clove, chopped
1/8 teaspoon whole cominos, crushed, or
   1/8 teaspoon ground cominos

1/4 cup chopped green chiles or 1 (4-oz.)
   can diced green chiles
2 cups diced processed cheese (16 oz.)
1 (10-1/2-oz.) can cream of celery soup
1/2 cup half-and-half or evaporated milk

Combine oil, onion, garlic and cominos in a 1-1/2-quart casserole. Cover with waxed paper; microwave on 100% (high) 2 to 3 minutes or until onion is transparent.

Add chiles, cheese and celery soup; stir to blend. Cover with waxed paper; microwave on 100% (high) 3 minutes or until cheese melts. Stir in half-and-half or milk. Cover with waxed paper; microwave on 50% (medium) 3 minutes. Serve hot as a dip or sauce. Mixture can be frozen for later use.

Variation

Omit cream of celery soup and reduce processed cheese to 1-1/2 cups. Use as a topping over warm corn tortillas.

Chiles Rellenos

Baked Stuffed Chiles

Long, wide green chiles work best for this recipe. Chiles Rellenos can also be stuffed with cooked ground beef, turkey, tuna, shrimp or refried beans.

Power level: high
Cooking time: 6 minutes
Servings: 3

6 whole roasted chiles, page 3, or
    1 (7-oz.) can whole green chiles
4 oz. mild Cheddar cheese, cut in
    6 (3" x 1/2") strips
3 eggs, separated
1/4 teaspoon cream of tartar, if desired
2 tablespoons all-purpose flour

1/2 teaspoon baking powder
1/8 teaspoon salt
1/8 teaspoon pepper
1/4 teaspoon paprika
2 tablespoons butter or margarine
1/2 cup shredded Cheddar cheese (2 oz.)

Cut a lengthwise slit along each chile pod; remove seeds. Leave stem on. Fill interior of each chile with a cheese strip. In a small bowl, beat egg whites until stiff, gradually adding cream of tartar to help stiffen egg whites, if desired.

In a separate bowl, combine egg yolks, flour, baking powder, salt, pepper and paprika; beat well. Fold egg-white mixture into yolk mixture. Pour egg batter in a shallow glass dish.

Place butter or margarine in a 12" x 8" casserole. Cover with waxed paper; microwave on 100% (high) 1-1/2 minutes. Dip chiles in egg batter; place chiles side by side in casserole. Microwave on 100% (high) 2 minutes. Turn chiles over with a spatula; microwave on 100% (high) 2 minutes. If batter is not set, turn chiles over; microwave on 100% (high) 1 minute or until batter is set.

Top chiles with shredded cheese; microwave on 100% (high) 45 seconds or until cheese melts. Rellenos are ready to serve.

Chile y Queso al Horno

Chile & Cheese Bake

Combining chiles and cheese gives this dish a great taste.

Power level: high
Cooking time: 8-1/2 minutes
Servings: 4

1/2 cup green-chile strips	1/2 teaspoon salt
1 cup shredded Cheddar cheese (4 oz.)	1/4 teaspoon paprika
2 eggs	3/4 cup fresh bread crumbs
1 cup half and half	2 tablespoons butter or margarine

Butter a 1-1/2-quart casserole. Using half the chile strips, make a layer of chiles in buttered dish. Top chile strips with half the cheese; set aside.

Beat eggs in a separate bowl; add half and half, salt and paprika. Blend well. Pour egg mixture over chiles and cheese. Top egg mixture with a layer of remaining chile strips.

Place bread crumbs in a small bowl; cut butter or margarine into bread crumbs. Sprinkle crumb mixture over chiles and cheese. Cover with waxed paper; microwave on 100% (high) 8 minutes, rotating dish after 4 minutes. Top chile dish with remaining cheese. Cover with waxed paper; microwave on 100% (high) 30 seconds or until cheese melts. To test for doneness, insert a wooden pick into center of dish. If it comes out clean, it is done. If more cooking is needed, cover with waxed paper; microwave on 100% (high) 1 minute. Let stand 5 minutes before serving.

Guacamole

Avocado Dip

Guacamole is used as a garnish for all types of Mexican dishes. Pick a soft avocado or see below for how to soften an avocado.

Servings: 1/2 to 3/4 cup

1 avocado
2 tablespoons chopped onion
1/4 cup Taco Sauce, page 7

Remove peel and seed from avocado; place avocado in a small bowl. Mash avocado with a fork. Add onion and Taco Sauce; stir to combine. Guacamole is ready to serve.

Tip

If avocados are just a little under-ripe, put them in the microwave on 50% (medium) 30 to 45 seconds, rotating after 15 to 20 seconds. Repeat process if needed.

To peel an avocado, cut it into 4 lengthwise sections cutting through to the pit. Peel each quarter of the avocado by pulling off the skin starting at the narrow end. The flesh should loosen from the pit. If not, use a knife to pry the flesh from the pit. Cut the avocado into 1/2-inch cubes or mash it. Try to prepare the avocado just before serving so it will not discolor. Lemon or lime juice can be squeezed over the avocado to help preserve its color.

Serrano Chutney

Serrano chiles are thin, dark-green chiles, about 2-inches long. These chiles can be quite hot.

Power level: high
Cooking time: 1 minute
Servings: about 1/2 cup

15 serrano chiles
2 slightly ripe tomatoes, chopped
2 tablespoons chopped onion

1 garlic clove, chopped
1 tablespoon sugar
Dash of ground cloves, if desired

Wash chiles and remove stems; finely chop chiles. Combine all ingredients in a glass bowl. Microwave on 100% (high) 1 minute. Serve hot or cold. This chutney goes well with meat dishes.

Tip

Slightly ripe tomatoes should have a combination of green, yellow and red skin color.

Drying Green Chiles

A wonderful way to use fresh chiles from your garden.

Power level: high, medium-high
Cooking time: 12 to 14 minutes
Servings: 3/4 cup

5 or 6 whole roasted chiles, page 3, or 6 canned whole green chiles

Cut a lengthwise slit along each chile; remove stems, seeds and membranes. Place chiles on paper towels to drain.

Line bottom of a 12" x 8" flat-bottom casserole with paper towels. Open slit chiles and place in lined dish; microwave on 70% (medium-high) 6 to 7 minutes. Remove chiles from dish by lifting paper towels; set chiles aside. Place fresh paper towels on bottom of casserole. Transfer chiles back into lined casserole. Microwave on 70% (medium-high) another 6 to 7 minutes. Dried chiles should have a paper-like texture. If chiles are not completely dried, repeat procedure.

The traditional way of drying roasted green chiles was to clean pods of stems and seeds; then thread pods on a string and hang them outside in a well-ventilated area. Drying can be quickly accomplished by using a microwave. After chiles have been dried, they can be used as a condiment or for Chile Pasado, page 22. They can also be frozen for later use.

Chile Pasado

Dried Green Chile

Serve this tasty condiment with your favorite meat dishes.

Power level: high, medium-high
Cooking time: 4 minutes
Servings: 1 cup

3/4 cup dried green chiles, page 21
1 cup water
2 tablespoons vegetable oil
1/4 cup chopped onion
1 garlic clove, chopped

1/8 teaspoon cilantro seeds, crushed
1/4 teaspoon dried leaf oregano, crushed
1 tomato, blanched, chopped, page 4
1/2 teaspoon salt

Break dried chiles into small pieces; place in a small bowl. Soak chiles in warm water 15 minutes or until softened. Drain and discard liquid; set chiles aside.

Combine oil, onion, garlic, cilantro and oregano in a 1-1/2-quart casserole. Cover with waxed paper; microwave on 100% (high) 2 minutes. Add soaked chiles, tomato and salt to onion mixture. Cover with waxed paper; microwave on 70% (medium-high) 2 minutes. Stir mixture well. Serve hot or cold.

Variation

Chile Pasado con Queso

Dried Green Chile with Cheese

Stir 1/2 cup shredded Monterey Jack cheese into 1 cup Chile Pasado. Microwave on 100% (high) 45 seconds to melt cheese. Stir well and serve.

Carne con Chile Pasado

Dried Green Chile with Meat

Serve with flour tortillas and Chile con Queso, page 16, for a quick and easy meal.

Power level: medium-high
Cooking time: 6 to 8 minutes
Servings: 3 cups

1 cup Chile Pasado, page 22
2 cups shredded cooked beef or pork, pages 86–88

Combine Chile Pasado and shredded meat in a 1-1/2-quart casserole. Cover with waxed paper; microwave on 70% (medium-high) 6 to 8 minutes or until heated through, stirring after 3 minutes.

❧ ❧ ❧

Chile pasado is dehydrated chile. The chile is dried after the growing season and used during winter months. Other dried vegetables and fruits are collectively called "orejones," meaning "long ears" because of their similarity to ears.

One popular dish made with dried chiles and dried squash is called "Orejones de Calabaza." The dehydrated squash and dried chiles are combined with corn to make a dish similar to succotash. The squash is first soaked and drained, then added to the prepared chile pasado with either canned or frozen corn.

Although green chiles dry well in a microwave oven, page 21, I have been unsuccessful in drying squash in a microwave. Dry squash by hanging it outside "clothesline style" or use a dehydrator.

Caldo de Chile Colorado Fresco

Fresh Red Chile Soup

I recommend using fresh red chiles. If they are not available, use dried red chiles.

Power level: high
Cooking time: 17 minutes
Servings: 4

6 fresh red chiles or 12 dried red chiles
3 cups water
1/2 teaspoon salt
1 tablespoon all-purpose flour
2 tablespoons butter or margarine

1/4 cup chopped onion
1 garlic clove, chopped
1/4 teaspoon ground cominos
1-1/2 cups shredded Monterey Jack
    cheese (6 oz.)

Roast and peel fresh chiles following method on page 3. Remove stems and seeds from chiles. In a blender, combine chiles, water, salt and flour. Process until smooth; set mixture aside.

Combine butter or margarine, onion, garlic and cominos in a small glass dish. Cover with waxed paper; microwave on 100% (high) 2 minutes. Combine red-chile mixture and onion mixture in a 2-1/2-quart casserole. Cover with waxed paper; microwave on 100% (high) 15 minutes, stirring after 7-1/2 minutes. Immediately stir in cheese. Serve hot.

Or, wash dried chiles thoroughly but do not remove stems. Soak pods overnight in 4 cups water. Or place dried pods in a large glass bowl; cover with 4 cups water. Microwave on 100% (high) 20 minutes, rearranging pods every 5 minutes. chile pods are ready when they are soft and limp. Allow to cool. Remove pods from liquid. Slit pods lengthwise; remove stems and seeds. With a spoon, scrape chile pulp from pods, placing pulp in a blender; add water, salt and flour. Process until mixture is smooth; set aside.

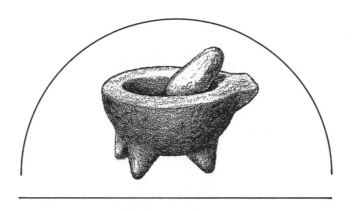

COMIDAS de MASA

Mexican cooking practices were largely adapted from native Indian techniques, such as the old method of grinding corn. Women would grind corn in a "metate" or volcanic concave stone, using a "mano," a cylindrical hand-held stone. The mano was usually selected by the individual user.

In our neighborhood, the smell of freshly baked flour tortillas was hard to hide from the army of children. I can recall somehow always being present when tortillas were being baked anytime at anyone's house. Watching the process was half the fun. Whoever was making the tortillas would take a ball of dough and rhythmically slap it from hand to hand, forming a big round tortilla. Our eyes would focus on the tortilla as it was being baked on the "comal" or hot griddle. We knew that eventually we would be handed a hot, buttered tortilla. The only problem was one tortilla wasn't enough. If we were told that we were only getting one, the process of snitching extras would begin.

Included in these recipes is a master mix for tortillas. I am sure you will find them a staple for many of the main-dish recipes.

Traditional etiquette among Mexican people was to use the tortilla as a spoon. My father had developed a special method of making "spoons" from the tortilla to use in eating Caldillo and Carne con Chile Colorado. He would tear a piece from a flour tortilla and form a "cucharita," Spanish for small spoon. He would roll the piece of tortilla into a cone and fold it shut at one end. The open end formed the spoon.

Flour Tortilla Mix

Save time by keeping this mix made ahead and available to use. It will make enough mix for several batches of tortillas.

Servings: about 10 cups

10 cups all-purpose flour
4 teaspoons baking powder
4 teaspoons salt
3/4 cup vegetable shortening

Combine flour, baking powder and salt in a bowl. Cut in shortening with a pastry blender or fork until mixture is the consistency of cornmeal. Place mixture in an airtight container. Store in a cool, dry place up to 3 months. Refrigerate for longer storage.

Flour Tortillas

Fresh flour tortillas make any meal special.

Servings: 12

3 cups Flour Tortilla Mix, page 26
1 cup warm water

Place tortilla mix in a medium bowl. Gradually add warm water, working mixture until it sticks together to form a ball. If dough is dry, add an additional 1 tablespoon warm water; then work dough. Repeat if necessary. Turn dough out onto a lightly floured board; knead 5 minutes. Cover dough with a damp cloth; let stand 30 minutes.

Divide dough into 12 pieces, forming each into a ball. On a lightly floured board, roll each ball into a thin circle of even thickness, about 8 inches in diameter. Stack tortillas, separating each with a piece of waxed paper.

Cook tortillas on a griddle or in an electric skillet. Heat ungreased griddle or skillet. When hot, cook each tortilla about 30 seconds or until bubbles begin to form in the tortilla. Flip tortilla over; cook about 30 seconds or until brown spots form. Stack cooked tortillas on a damp cloth; wrap to keep them soft. Tortillas are ready to use or store in a closed plastic bag in the refrigerator 4 to 7 days.

Variation

Microwave Tortillas

Heat a microwave browning dish on 100% (high) 5 minutes. Place a tortilla on the hot browning dish; microwave on 100% (high) 35 seconds. Turn tortilla over; microwave on 100% (high) another 35 seconds. Remove tortilla; place on a damp cloth. Fold cloth over tortilla to retain moisture and heat. Repeat for remaining tortillas, including stacking them in the damp cloth. It may be necessary to reheat the browning dish every third or fourth tortilla.

Tamales

Tamales derive their origin from corn dishes dating back to days of the Aztec Empire. Making tamales was always a community project in our neighborhood. I remember watching women preparing tamales for the church bazaar. They would station themselves around the kitchen to make an assembly line, each doing a particular task. Several steps were required in making tamales: softening corn husks, dough preparation, filling preparation and cooking. The conventional cooking method took about 1 hour, but cooking tamales today in a microwave takes only 10 minutes!

I was too young to keep count, but I recall seeing many paper bags, each filled with a dozen tamales to be sold at the church bazaar. Tamales made for the bazaar were always red-chile tamales because they were everyone's favorite. Contrary to convention, I particularly liked the Tamales Dulces or Sweet Tamales.

Four basic tamale recipes are given in this book. However, there is a wide variety of tamale recipes in Mexican cuisine which can be made in the microwave using the same methods of these recipes.

The type of tamale determines the selection of the dough and filling. Red-Chile Tamales are made with red-chile filling and red-chile-based dough. Green-Chile Tamales are made with green-chile filling and green-chile-based dough. Sweet tamales are made with sweet filling and sweet dough. Use the appropriate dough and filling when making your favorite tamales.

Tamales de Chile Colorado Dough

Red-Chile Tamale Dough

This flavorful fresh corn dough is used for making your own tamales.

Servings: 36

3/4 cup Chile Colorado, page 8, or 3/4 cup
    beef broth
1 (10-oz.) pkg. frozen whole-kernel corn,
    thawed
2 (14-1/2-oz.) cans golden or white
    hominy, drained

3/4 cup lard or vegetable shortening
2 teaspoons salt
2 teaspoons baking powder
2-1/2 cups white cornmeal

In a blender or food processor, combine Chile Colorado or broth, corn and hominy; process until pureed. You may need to do this in batches, depending on the size of your equipment.

In a large bowl, combine pureed chile mixture, lard or shortening, salt, baking powder and cornmeal. Using an electric mixer, beat until dough is smooth. Dough is ready to use.

This recipe makes a Chile-Colorado-based dough for red-chile tamales. Tamales can be made with a fresh corn dough or a masa harina dough. Masa harina is a ground corn mixture and can be purchased at most supermarkets.

Masa Harina Dough

Servings: 36

Fresh dough enhances any dish it is used in.

1 cup lard or vegetable shortening	1/2 cup Chile Colorado, page 8, or
3 cups masa harina	1/2 cup beef broth
1 teaspoon salt	1-1/4 cups water

Beat lard or shortening with an electric mixer until creamy. Add masa harina, salt, Chile Colorado or broth and water. Beat until dough is smooth. Dough is ready to use.

Variation

Tamales de Chile Verde Dough

Green-Chile Tamale Dough

Substitute Salsa Para Enchiladas Verdes, page 10, or beef broth for Chile Colorado.

Tamales de Chile Colorado

Red-Chile Tamales

Great-tasting tamales that are easy to prepare.

Power level: high
Cooking time: 10 minutes per dozen
Servings: about 36

1/2 lb. dry corn husks
2 cups Carne con Chile Colorado, page 78, for filling
Tamales de Chile Colorado Dough, page 29, Fresh Corn Dough or Masa Harina Dough,
    page 30

Soak corn husks overnight in water or until soft. Prepare dough and filling, dicing meat into smaller pieces.

Tamales can be cooked by a standard microwave method or by using a microwave pressure cooker.

For conventional microwave method, open corn husks; if one husk is not large enough for a tamale, then take 2 and overlap them before spreading on dough. Spread with 2 tablespoons tamale dough at center of husk. Top with 1 tablespoon tamale filling. Make tamales no more than 4-inches long or so they will stand in your cooking container. Fold and wrap each tamale as follows: fold bottom of husk over dough and filling, fold sides together, then take a thin lengthwise piece of husk and tie top of tamale. Make sure tamale is tied tightly and dough is not exposed, otherwise dough will dry out.

Stand 12 tamales in a 2-quart glass measuring cup; cover with plastic wrap. Pierce plastic wrap with a fork so steam will vent during cooking. Microwave on 100% (high) 10 minutes, rotating dish after 5 minutes. Let stand 5 minutes before serving. Tamales can be stored in a freezer up to 3 months. Thaw and reheat for serving.

For a microwave pressure cooker, fill tamales as above. Fold and wrap each tamale as follows: fold bottom of husk over dough and filling, then fold left side and top of husk over dough and filling. Roll up tamale toward the right edge of husk. Take a thin lengthwise strip of husk and wrap around the middle of the tamale roll; tie securely. Place tamales standing on end, side by side, in a microwave pressure cooker. To keep tamales from drying out, cut a piece of foil the size of the diameter of the pressure cooker; place over tamales.

Caution: Some microwave ovens may not tolerate any metal during operation. Check your microwave oven owner's manual before using foil.

Close pressure cooker; put on pressure regulator weight. Microwave on 100% (high) 10 minutes. Let pressure cooker stand with pressure 5 minutes. If pressure cooker has a pressure-indicating gauge or stem, allow standing time to be the time it takes for indicator to show pressure has dropped. Remove pressure-regulator weight; open pressure cooker. Tamales are ready to serve. Tamales can be stored in a freezer up to 3 months. Thaw and reheat for serving.

Tamales de Chile Verde

Green-Chile Tamales

Red-chile tamales are the traditional tamale. For variety, try Green-Chile Tamales.

Power level: medium, high
Cooking time: 30 to 45 minutes for filling
                  10 minutes per dozen
Servings: about 36

1/2 lb. dry corn husks
Tamales de Chile Verde Dough, page 30
1-1/2 lbs. pork or beef roast

1/4 cup water
1 cup Salsa Para Enchiladas Verdes,
    page 10

Soak corn husks overnight in water or until soft. Prepare dough.

Shredded meat for tamale filling can be made by a conventional microwave method, in an oven-cooking bag or in a microwave pressure cooker. Oven-cooking bags or a microwave pressure cooker help keep meat moist and tender.

For conventional microwave method, place roast in a casserole; add 1/4 cup water. Cover dish with a lid; microwave on 50% (medium) 25 to 30 minutes per pound, turning meat over after half the cooking time. Cool roast.

If using an oven-cooking bag, place 1 tablespoon all-purpose flour in cooking bag; this will help keep bag from bursting during cooking. Place roast and 1/4 cup water in bag. Place bag in a 2-inch or deeper casserole, making sure bag does not hang over edge of dish. Close bag using string or a rubber band; do not use a metal twist. Pierce bag right below where it is tied so steam can vent during cooking. Make sure neck of bag is upright so liquid does not leak from vent holes. Microwave on 50% (medium) 25 to 30 minutes per pound, turning bag over after half the cooking time. Cool roast.

For a microwave pressure cooker, place roast and 1/2 cup water in microwave pressure cooker. To keep roast from over-browning, cover with foil as described for covering tamales, page 32.

Close pressure cooker; put on pressure-regulator weight. Microwave on 100% (high) 30 minutes. Let pressure cooker stand with pressure 10 minutes. If pressure cooker has a pressure-indicating gauge or stem, allow standing time to be time it takes for indicator to show pressure has dropped. Remove pressure-regulator weight; open pressure cooker. Cool roast.

To complete filling, shred cooled roast by pulling it apart with a fork or cut roast into strips. Shred enough pork or beef to make 1 cup for tamale filling. Add 1 cup Salsa Para Enchiladas Verdes to shredded meat.

Fill and cook tamales by the conventional microwave method or in a microwave pressure cooker, pages 31–32. Serve immediately or freeze up to 3 months. Thaw and reheat to serve.

Variations

Tamales con Queso

Omit shredded pork or beef. Sprinkle 1 tablespoon shredded cheese on salsa filling and add 1 ripe olive, cut in half, to complete filling for each tamale. Follow recipe as above.

Tamales de Pollo

Omit shredded pork or beef. Substitute 1 cup shredded cooked chicken. Combine chicken with 1 cup Salsa Para Enchiladas Verdes, page 10. Follow recipe as above. Sprinkle shredded cheese over filling before folding tamale, if desired.

Tamales Dulces

Sweet Tamales

Sweet tamales are served as dessert, often at festive occasions.

Power level: high
Cooking time: 4 minutes for filling
              10 minutes per dozen
Servings: 24

1/2 lb. corn husks
1 (20-oz.) can crushed pineapple
3 cups masa harina
1 cup lard or vegetable shortening
1 cup sugar
1 teaspoon salt

1/2 cup sugar
1/2 cup raisins
1/4 cup water
1/4 teaspoon ground cinnamon
2 tablespoons cornstarch
1/2 cup pecan pieces, if desired

Soak corn husks overnight in water or until soft. For dough, drain pineapple juice into a 2-cup measure. Add enough water to make 1-1/4 cups liquid. Combine masa harina, lard or shortening, 1 cup sugar, salt and pineapple liquid in a large bowl. Beat with an electric mixer until a soft dough is formed; set dough aside.

To prepare filling, combine drained crushed pineapple, 1/2 cup sugar, raisins, water, cinnamon, cornstarch and nuts, if desired, in a glass bowl. Cover with waxed paper; microwave on 100% (high) 4 minutes, stirring mixture after 2 minutes. Set filling aside.

Fill and cook tamales by the conventional microwave method or in a microwave pressure cooker, pages 31–32. Serve after cooking or store in freezer up to 3 months. Thaw and reheat to serve.

Rolled Enchiladas

Here's a quick way to prepare those always-favorite enchiladas.

Power level: high, medium-high
Cooking time: 14 to 18 minutes
Servings: 6

3 cups cooked Chile Colorado, page 8
1 lb. ground beef
12 (6-inch) corn tortillas
2 tablespoons vegetable oil
2-1/2 cups shredded Cheddar cheese
    (10 oz.)

1/2 cup chopped onion
2 cups shredded lettuce
1/2 cup chopped tomatoes

Place Chile Colorado in a flat-bottom casserole; microwave on 100% (high) 2 minutes; set aside. Crumble ground beef into a 1-1/2-quart casserole or microwave browning dish. Cover with waxed paper; microwave on 100% (high) 5 to 6 minutes, stirring after 3 minutes. Meat is done when it is no longer pink. Drain off fat; set meat aside.

Rub both sides of each tortilla with oil; place in 2 stacks of 6 tortillas each. To soften tortillas, wrap each stack in waxed paper; microwave 1 stack on 100% (high) 50 seconds. Remove tortillas; repeat for remaining stack.

Grease a 12" x 8" flat-bottom casserole. Dip each softened tortilla into chile sauce. Spoon 2 heaping tablespoons meat in center of a tortilla; sprinkle a little cheese and onion on top. Starting at one side, roll tortilla tightly; place seam-side down in greased casserole. Repeat for all tortillas. Pour remaining sauce over filled and rolled tortillas. Sprinkle with remaining onion and cheese.

Cover with waxed paper; microwave on 70% (medium-high) 5 to 8 minutes or until enchiladas are hot and bubbly, rotating dish after 3 minutes. Let stand 1 minute. Garnish with lettuce and tomatoes. Serve immediately.

Variation

Stacked Enchiladas

Follow recipe, opposite page, except do not roll tortillas. Leave tortillas flat and stack in flat-bottom casserole. To do this, dip each tortilla in chile sauce; top with meat, cheese and onion. Make 2 stacks of 6 tortillas each. Cover with waxed paper; microwave on 70% (medium-high) 5 to 8 minutes or until enchiladas are hot and bubbly, rotating dish after 3 minutes. Let stand 1 minute. Garnish with lettuce and tomatoes. Serve immediately. Top tortilla stacks with Microwave Eggs, page 61, if desired. Serve immediately.

My mother served red-chile enchiladas at least once a week. They were also particularly popular as a pre-game meal for the football crowd. She would top the stack of enchiladas with a fried egg. This is the traditional way of serving enchiladas in Southern New Mexico.

There is a degree of regionalism in Mexican cuisine between Texas-Coahuila or Tex-Mex, New Mexico-Chihuahua, Arizona-Sonora, and California-Baja, but in all cases, the chile remains the dominant ingredient. One of the distinctions between the Chihuahuan and Sonoran cuisines is that a burrito in New Mexico is a burro in Arizona.

Enchiladas Verdes

Green Enchiladas

Tortillas are dipped in green-chile sauce and stacked one on top of another.

Power level: medium-high, high
Cooking time: 10 to 13 minutes
Servings: 4

**2 cups Salsa Para Enchiladas Verdes,
   page 10**
12 (6-inch) corn tortillas
2 tablespoons vegetable oil
**2-1/2 cups shredded Cheddar cheese (10
   oz.)**

1/2 cup chopped onion
1 cup shredded lettuce
1/2 cup chopped tomatoes

Pour enchilada sauce in a flat-bottom casserole. Cover with waxed paper; microwave on 70% (medium-high) 3 minutes. Set sauce aside.

Rub both sides of each tortilla with oil; place in 2 stacks of 6 tortillas each. To soften tortillas, wrap each stack in waxed paper; microwave 1 stack on 100% (high) 50 seconds. Remove tortillas; repeat for remaining stack.

Grease a 12" x 8" flat-bottom casserole. Dip each softened tortilla in Salsa Para Enchiladas Verdes. Place tortilla in greased casserole; sprinkle with cheese and onion. Top with another tortilla. Repeat alternating tortilla, cheese and onion, building 2 stacks of 6 tortillas each. Pour remaining sauce over tortillas.

Cover with waxed paper; microwave on 70% (medium-high) 5 to 8 minutes or until cheese melts, rotating dish after 3 minutes. Garnish with lettuce and tomatoes. Top tortilla stacks with Microwave Eggs, page 61, if desired. Serve immediately.

Variations

Sour-Cream Enchiladas

After heating green-chile sauce, stir in 1 cup dairy sour cream. Continue as directed for Green Enchiladas.

Enchiladas de Pollo

Chicken Enchiladas

Stir 2 cups shredded cooked chicken and 1 (10-1/2-oz.) can cream of chicken soup into enchilada sauce. Continue as directed for Green Enchiladas. This is an excellent way to use leftover cooked chicken.

Burritos

Burros, as they are sometimes called, are made by filling a large flour tortilla with a bean or meat mixture, or sometimes both.

Power level: high
Cooking time: 13 to 16 minutes
Servings: 6

1 lb. ground beef	**1/4 teaspoon dried leaf oregano, crushed**
2 tablespoons vegetable oil	**12 (10-inch) flour tortillas**
2 tablespoons red chile powder	**1 (16-oz.) can refried beans**
1/4 cup chopped onion	**1-1/2 cups shredded Cheddar cheese**
1 garlic clove, chopped	**(6 oz.)**
1/2 teaspoon salt	

Crumble ground beef into a 2-quart casserole. Cover with waxed paper; microwave on 100% (high) 4 to 5 minutes, stirring after 2 minutes. Meat is done when it is no longer pink. Drain off fat; set meat aside.

Combine oil, chile powder, onion, garlic, salt and oregano in a 1-1/2-quart casserole. Cover with waxed paper; microwave on 100% (high) 2 minutes. Add cooked ground beef, blending well. Cover with waxed paper; microwave on 100% (high) 3 to 4 minutes.

Moisten both sides of each tortilla with water; place in 2 stacks of 6 tortillas each. To soften tortillas, wrap each stack in waxed paper; microwave 1 stack on 100% (high) 50 seconds. Remove tortillas; repeat for remaining stack.

Grease a 12" x 8" flat-bottom casserole. Spread 2 tablespoons refried beans on a softened tortilla. Top with 2 tablespoons meat mixture. Sprinkle with a little cheese. Starting at one side, roll tortilla tightly; place seam-side down in greased casserole. Repeat for all tortillas. Cover with waxed paper; microwave on 100% (high) 2 to 3 minutes or until hot through. Serve immediately.

Tacos de Carne

Beef Tacos

Tacos are fried corn tortillas folded in half, filled with meat and topped with cheese and condiments.

Power level: high, medium-high
Cooking time: 10 to 11 minutes
Servings: 6

1-1/2 lbs. ground beef
1/4 cup chopped onion
3 tablespoons Taco Seasoning Mix, page
    7, or 1 (1-1/4-oz.) pkg. taco seasoning
    mix
1 (8-oz.) can tomato sauce
12 Taco Shells, page 49, or commercial
    shells

1-1/2 cups shredded Cheddar cheese
    (6 oz.)
2 cups shredded lettuce
1 cup chopped tomatoes
1 cup Taco Sauce, page 7

Crumble ground beef into a 2-quart casserole. Blend in onion. Cover with waxed paper; microwave on 100% (high) 4 minutes, stirring after 2 minutes. Drain off fat. Stir in taco seasoning mix and tomato sauce. Cover with waxed paper; microwave on 70% (medium-high) 5 to 6 minutes, stirring after 3 minutes. Spoon cooked meat mixture into each taco shell, placing filled shells upright in a flat-bottom casserole. Top with cheese. Microwave on 100% (high) 1 minute or until cheese melts. Garnish with lettuce and tomatoes. Serve hot with Taco Sauce.

Tacos de Pollo

Chicken Tacos

A great way to use cooked chicken and a welcome change from the traditional beef taco.

Power level: high
Cooking time: 3 minutes
Servings: 6

3/4 cup chopped onion
2 tablespoons vegetable oil
3 cups shredded cooked chicken
12 Taco Shells, page 49, or commercial
   shells

1-1/2 cups shredded Cheddar cheese
   (6 oz.)
2 cups shredded lettuce
1 cup chopped tomatoes
1 cup Taco Sauce, page 7

Combine 1/4 cup onion and oil in a 1-1/2-quart casserole. Cover with waxed paper; microwave on 100% (high) 2 minutes. Stir in cooked chicken; spoon mixture into taco shells; place filled shells upright in a flat-bottom casserole. Top with cheese. Microwave on 100% (high) 1 minute or until cheese melts. Sprinkle with lettuce, tomatoes and remaining 1/2 cup onion. Serve with Taco Sauce.

Flautas

Flautas are a variation of tacos.

Power level: high
Cooking time: 14-1/2 minutes
Servings: 4 to 6

1-1/2 lbs. ground beef
3 tablespoons Taco Seasoning Mix, page 7, or 1 (1-1/4-oz.) pkg. taco seasoning mix

12 (6-inch) corn tortillas
4 tablespoons vegetable oil
1-1/2 cups shredded Cheddar cheese (6 oz.)

Crumble ground beef into a 2-quart casserole. Cover with waxed paper; microwave on 100% (high) 5 minutes, stirring after 2-1/2 minutes. Drain off fat; stir in seasoning mix. Set mixture aside.

Rub both sides of each tortilla with oil, using about 2 tablespoons oil; place in 2 stacks of 6 tortillas each. To soften tortillas, wrap each stack in waxed paper; microwave 1 stack on 100% (high) 50 seconds. Remove tortillas; repeat for remaining stack.

Pour remaining 2 tablespoons oil in a 12" x 8" flat-bottom casserole. Cover with waxed paper; microwave on 100% (high) 1 minute. Spoon about 2 tablespoons cooked meat mixture onto a softened tortilla. Roll tortilla tightly; place seam-side down in casserole. Repeat for all tortillas. Cover with waxed paper; microwave on 100% (high) 4 minutes or until tortillas are crisp, rotating dish after 2 minutes.

Turn flautas over with a spatula. Cover with waxed paper; microwave on 100% (high) 2 minutes. Sprinkle flautas with cheese; microwave on 100% (high) 30 seconds or until cheese melts. Flautas may be served with a variety of toppings, including guacamole, shredded lettuce, chopped tomatoes and your choice of salsa.

Tostadas

Tostadas are flat, crisp corn tortillas topped with a tasty bean mixture.

Power level: high
Cooking time: 2 minutes each
Servings: 4

8 (6-inch) corn tortillas
2 tablespoons vegetable oil
1 cup Refried Beans, page 69, or
    1/2 (16-oz.) can refried beans, heated
1-1/2 cups shredded Cheddar cheese
    (6 oz.)

2 cups shredded lettuce
1 cup coarsely chopped tomatoes
1/2 cup chopped onion
1 cup Taco Sauce, page 7

Rub both sides of each tortilla lightly with oil; place on waxed paper. Microwave each tortilla on 100% (high) 1-1/2 minutes or until crisp. Spread 1 to 2 tablespoons beans on a tortilla. Cover with waxed paper; microwave on 100% (high) 30 seconds. Top with cheese, lettuce, tomatoes, onion and Taco Sauce. Repeat for each remaining tortilla. Serve immediately.

Quesadillas

Cheese-Filled Tortillas

Here's a quick and easy snack, great for children to learn to prepare.

Power level: high
Cooking time: 1-1/2 minutes each
Servings: 6

12 (6-inch) corn or (8-inch) flour tortillas
2 tablespoons vegetable oil
2 cups shredded Monterey Jack or Cheddar cheese (8 oz.)

Rub both sides of each tortilla lightly with oil; place on waxed paper or a paper plate. Microwave each tortilla on 100% (high) 45 seconds. Sprinkle cheese on hot tortilla; fold tortilla in half. Microwave on 100% (high) 35 seconds or until cheese melts. Repeat for each tortilla. Serve immediately.

Quesadillas are a favorite cheese-filled tortilla of mine. Traditionally, Quesadillas are traditionally made with goat cheese called "asadero." I substitute Monterey Jack or mild Cheddar cheese for the asadero. My children quickly learned to prepare Quesadillas in the microwave.

Chile Con Queso Nachos

Cheese Dip Nachos

Children of all ages enjoy nachos as a snack or party appetizer.

Power level: high, medium-high
Cooking time: 7 minutes
Servings: 4 to 6

16 (6-inch) corn tortillas, prepared as chips, page 50, or 1 (11-oz.) pkg. tortilla chips
1-1/2 cups Chile con Queso, page 16

Prepare microwave tortilla chips and Chile con Queso. Place chips in a bowl; pour hot Chile con Queso over chips. Serve immediately.

Cheese Nachos

Having a party? Here's a great party snack.

Power level: medium-high
Cooking time: 30 seconds per serving
Servings: 4 to 6

16 (6-inch) corn tortillas, prepared as chips, page 50, or 1 (11-oz.) pkg. tortilla chips
2 cups Refried Beans, page 69, or 1 (16-oz.) can refried beans
2 cups shredded Cheddar cheese (8 oz.)
1 cup Taco Sauce, page 7

Prepare microwave tortilla chips. Spread beans on each tortilla chip. Top with cheese. Place 12 chips on a paper plate; microwave on 70% (medium-high) 30 seconds or until cheese melts. Repeat for remaining chips. Pour Taco Sauce over chips. Serve immediately.

Cheese Crisps

Tasty flour tortillas topped with cheese.

Power level: high
Cooking time: 70 seconds each
Servings: 4

4 (8-inch) flour tortillas
2 tablespoons butter or margarine
1 cup shredded Cheddar cheese (4 oz.)
1/4 cup Taco Sauce, page 7

Spread both sides of each tortilla with butter or margarine. Place 1 tortilla on waxed paper or a paper plate; microwave on 100% (high) 40 seconds. Sprinkle hot tortilla with 1/4 cup cheese; microwave on 100% (high) 30 seconds or until cheese melts. Repeat for each remaining tortilla. Serve hot with Taco Sauce.

Compuestas

Cheese Crisps Deluxe

Cheese crisps, also known as tostadas, can be dressed up with a variety of toppings.

Power level: high
Cooking time: 1-1/2 minutes each
Servings: 2 to 4

4 (8-inch) flour tortillas
2 tablespoons butter or margarine
1 cup Refried Beans, page 69, or 1/2
    (16-oz.) can refried beans
1 cup shredded Cheddar cheese (4 oz.)

1 cup Taco Sauce, page 7
1/2 cup shredded lettuce
1/2 cup chopped tomatoes
1/4 cup sliced ripe olives
1/4 cup chopped onion

Spread both sides of each tortilla lightly with butter or margarine. Place 1 tortilla on waxed paper or a paper plate; microwave on 100% (high) 40 seconds. Spread hot tortilla with 1/4 cup beans; sprinkle with 1/4 cup cheese. Microwave on 100% (high) 30 to 40 seconds or until cheese melts. Top with 1/4 cup Taco Sauce, 2 tablespoons each of lettuce and tomatoes, and 1 tablespoon each of olives and onion. Repeat for each remaining tortilla. Serve hot.

Taco Shells

The trick to making taco shells is to microwave the tortilla in the shape of a shell.

Power level: high
Cooking time: 3 to 5 minutes
Servings: 5 taco shells

5 (6-inch) corn tortillas
Vegetable oil

Method 1

Rub both sides of each tortilla lightly with oil; stack tortillas. To soften tortillas, wrap stack with waxed paper; microwave on 100% (high) 50 seconds. While tortillas are soft, fold each tortilla over the rim of a large bowl. Microwave on 100% (high) 3 to 4 minutes, turning bowl each minute. Desired softness or crispness of the tortilla will determine length of cooking time. Remove tortillas from rim of bowl; they should be in the half-circle shape of a taco shell.

Fill taco shells with your favorite fillings; top with lettuce, cheese, chopped tomatoes and salsa.

Method 2

Taco shells can also be formed using a ceramic taco server. Be sure the taco server is microwave safe. These can be purchased at kitchenware and department stores.

Using as many tortillas as the taco server will hold, soften as above. While tortillas are soft, place each in a slot of the taco server with the tortilla edges facing upward. If tortillas are too limp, support them with wooden picks so they do not collapse or fall over in the server. Microwave on 100% (high) 2 to 3 minutes, turning taco server each minute. Desired softness or crispness of the tortilla will determine length of cooking time.

Tortilla Chips

Homemade are the best!

Power level: high
Cooking time: 3 minutes per serving
Servings: 1-1/2 cups

6 (6-inch) corn tortillas
4 teaspoons vegetable oil
Salt to taste

Cut each tortilla into 6 pie-shaped wedges. Place half the tortilla wedges in a single layer in a 12" x 8" flat-bottom casserole; add 2 teaspoons oil. Coat wedges with oil; microwave on 100% (high) 3 minutes. Drain wedges on paper towels; salt to taste. Repeat for remaining tortilla wedges. Serve warm.

Variation

Seasoned Tortilla Chips

Prepare chips as above. Place chips in a large plastic bag; add 3 tablespoons Taco Seasoning Mix, page 7, or 1 (1-1/4-oz.) pkg. taco seasoning mix. Shake bag lightly until chips are well coated. Shake off excess seasoning. Serve immediately.

Tip

If counting calories, instead of coating with oil, moisten each tortilla wedge with water. Microwave as above.

Crispas

Crispies

A sweet, cinnamon-flavored crisp tortilla that goes great when served at parties.

Power level: high
Cooking time: 2 minutes per plate
Servings: 6

6 (8-inch) flour tortillas
2 tablespoons vegetable oil
1/2 cup sugar
1 teaspoon ground cinnamon

Rub both sides of each tortilla lightly with oil. Cut each tortilla in 6 pie-shaped wedges.

Grease bottom of a 12" x 8" flat-bottom casserole. Place 8 or 9 oiled tortilla wedges in greased casserole; microwave on 100% (high) 1 minute. Turn wedges over; microwave on 100% (high) 1 minute or until crisp.

Combine sugar and cinnamon in a small bowl; dip each hot tortilla wedge in sugar mixture. Repeat cooking process for remaining tortilla wedges; then dip each in sugar mixture.

Crispies can also be prepared by using a microwave browning dish. Heat browning dish on 100% (high) 4 minutes. Place 8 tortilla wedges in hot browning dish; microwave on 100% (high) 1 minute. Turn wedges over; microwave on 100% (high) 1 minute. When tortilla wedges are crisp, dip in sugar mixture.

Chimichangas

Microwave-Crisp Burritos

Chimichangas are a popular deep-fried burrito.

Power level: high
Cooking time: 5 minutes
Servings: 5

5 (8-inch) flour tortillas
Vegetable oil or water
3/4 cup filling, such as cooked, shredded
    beef or pork, pages 86–87; Refried Beans,
    page 69; or ground beef

1/3 cup Chile Colorado, page 8, or
    Salsa Para Enchiladas Verdes,
    page 10
1/2 cup shredded Cheddar cheese (2 oz.)
Condiments of your choice

Rub both sides of each tortilla lightly with oil or water; stack tortillas. To soften tortillas, wrap stack with waxed paper; microwave on 100% (high) 50 seconds. Spread 2 tablespoons filling of choice in center of each tortilla; top with 1 tablespoon sauce of choice. Sprinkle with cheese.

Fold bottom edge of tortilla up; fold left, then right sides over filling; then fold top of tortilla down. Brush outer surface of chimichanga with vegetable oil. Repeat for remaining chimichangas.

Heat a microwave browning dish on 100% (high) 4 minutes. Place 5 chimichangas in hot browning dish; microwave on 100% (high) 4 minutes or until crisp, turning after 2 minutes and rotating dish. Serve with your favorite condiments.

Prepared in the microwave, they have fewer calories than when deep-fried.Chimichangas are delicious topped with sour cream, Guacamole or Chile con Queso. It wasn't until I moved to Arizona that I understood what a Chimichanga was. Since my first taste of a fried burrito or Chimichanga, I have become addicted. My recipe is a rendition of the Arizona Chimichanga.

Caldo de Tortillas

Tortilla Soup

A great soup to begin any meal.

Power level: high
Cooking time: 12 minutes
Servings: 4 cups

2 tablespoons vegetable oil
1/4 cup chopped onion
1 garlic clove, chopped
1/4 teaspoon ground cominos
4 cups chicken broth or 4 chicken bouillon cubes dissolved in 4 cups hot water

5 (6-inch) corn tortillas, cut in 1-inch
pieces
1/4 cup chopped green chiles
Salt to taste
2 tablespoons chopped fresh cilantro
or parsley

Combine oil, onion, garlic and cominos in a 2-quart glass bowl. Cover with waxed paper; microwave on 100% (high) 2 minutes. Add broth, tortillas and chiles to onion mixture. Cover with waxed paper; microwave on 100% (high) 10 minutes, stirring after 5 minutes. Season to taste. Garnish with cilantro or parsley. Serve hot.

Gorditas

Little Flat Tortillas

Top these appetizers with your favorite filling.

Power level: high, medium-high
Cooking time: 12 to 14 minutes
Servings: 12

2-1/2 cups masa harina
1 teaspoon salt
1 teaspoon baking soda
2 tablespoons lard or vegetable
    shortening
1-1/3 cups warm water
2 cups filling, such as Refried Beans,
    page 69; Machaca, pages 86–87; Carne con
    Chile Colorado, page 78; or Taco filling,
    pages 41–42

1/2 cup Taco Sauce, page 7
3/4 cup shredded Cheddar cheese (3 oz.)
1 cup shredded lettuce

Combine masa harina, salt and baking soda in a medium bowl. Cut in lard or shortening with a pastry blender or fork until mixture is the consistency of cornmeal. Blend in warm water to make a soft dough. If dough is dry, gradually add 1 tablespoon warm water until dough is easy to work. Repeat if necessary. Divide dough into 12 equal balls. Moisten hands. Flatten each ball with your hands to 3/8-inch thickness and 3-inches in diameter.

Hold flattened dough in palm of one hand; turn up edge of dough with other hand, making small rim. Repeat for remaining dough pieces.

Heat a microwave browning dish at 100% (high) 4 minutes. Place 6 gorditas toward edges of hot browning dish. Microwave on 70% (medium-high) 6 to 7 minutes, turning dish after 3 minutes. Gorditas are done when underside begins to brown. Place gorditas on a rack to cool. Reheat browning dish; repeat process for remaining gorditas.

Top each Gordita with 2 to 3 tablespoons filling of your choice. Top with Taco Sauce, cheese and lettuce. Serve immediately.

Variation

Chalupas

Little Canoes

These are Gorditas formed in the shape of little canoes. To make, flatten dough into an oval shape; pinch ends up to form a canoe. Microwave as above; add filling of your choice.

Pan de Maíz

Mexican Corn Bread

Corn bread is a tasty treat with beans and makes a real hearty meal.

Power level: medium, high
Cooking time: 10 to 11 minutes
Servings: 8

1 cup cornmeal
1/2 cup all-purpose flour
1 tablespoon baking powder
1 teaspoon salt
1 (8-1/2-oz.) can cream-style corn
1/4 cup vegetable oil

2 eggs
1/4 cup chopped green chiles or
   1 (4-oz.) can diced green chiles
1 cup shredded mild Cheddar cheese
   (4 oz.)

Combine cornmeal, flour, baking powder and salt in a bowl. Stir in corn, oil, eggs, chiles and cheese. Grease a microwave-safe ring mold or a round, glass cake dish. Place an inverted custard cup in center of cake dish. Pour batter into greased mold or cake dish. Microwave on 50% (medium) 5 minutes, turning after 2-1/2 minutes. Microwave on 100% (high) an additional 5 to 6 minutes, turning dish after 2-1/2 minutes. Let stand 5 minutes. Corn bread is done when a wooden pick inserted in center comes out clean. Serve warm with butter.

COMIDAS de HUEVOS

"Desayuno," or breakfast as known in the Southwest, was a very important meal in my family. I remember my dad having eggs with chorizo or scrambled eggs with green chile, never leaving out the hot tortilla.

Chorizo sausage originated in Spain. The chorizo my mother bought was pork sausage heavily seasoned with red chile and other Mexican seasonings. The outer casing was peeled before the filling could be fried.

My favorite egg dish has always been Huevos Rancheros con Chile Colorado. I place a flour tortilla on a plate, then top it with cooked huevos and Chile Colorado.

Many spices and ingredients are added to eggs in Mexican dishes. Eggs become a complete meal when eaten with beans, rice, tortillas and your favorite salsa.

Huevos Rancheros con Chile Colorado

Ranch-Style Eggs with Red Chile

Simply delicious served over a flour tortilla; my favorite way to have eggs.

Power level: high, medium-high
Cooking time: 4 to 5 minutes
Servings: 2

1 cup Chile Colorado, page 8
1 tablespoon vegetable oil
2 eggs

Combine Chile Colorado and oil in a 9-inch glass pie plate. Cover with waxed paper; microwave on 100% (high) 3 minutes. Carefully break eggs into chile mixture; try to avoid breaking egg yolks. With a wooden pick, pierce each egg yolk to prevent bursting when cooking. Spoon chile over eggs. Cover with waxed paper; microwave on 70% (medium-high) 45 seconds per egg, rotating dish after 25 seconds. If eggs are not completely cooked, microwave on 70% (medium-high) another 30 seconds or until eggs are cooked. Season to taste. Serve immediately.

Huevos Rancheros con Chile Verde

Ranch-Style Eggs with Green Chile

Serve these eggs for breakfast with corn tortillas and refried beans.

Power level: high, medium-high
Cooking time: 4 to 5 minutes
Servings: 2

1 tablespoon vegetable oil	2 eggs
2 tablespoons chopped onion	1/4 cup green chile strips
2 tablespoons chopped bell pepper	1 tablespoon water
1/2 garlic clove, chopped	1/4 cup shredded Cheddar cheese (1 oz.)

Combine oil, onion, bell pepper and garlic in a 9-inch glass pie plate. Cover with waxed paper; microwave on 100% (high) 2 minutes. Carefully break eggs into onion mixture; try to avoid breaking egg yolks. With a wooden pick, pierce each egg yolk to prevent bursting when cooking. Top eggs with chile strips; add 1 tablespoon water. Cover with waxed paper; microwave on 70% (medium-high) 2 to 3 minutes or until eggs are cooked. Top with cheese. Season to taste. Serve immediately.

Torta de Huevo Española

Spanish Omelet

Don't know what to prepare for breakfast? Try this delicious omelet. Cooked bacon or sausage can also be added with the cheese.

Power level: high
Cooking time: 4-1/2 minutes
Servings: 2

2 tablespoons butter or margarine	**2 tablespoons chopped green chiles**
2 tablespoons chopped onion	**2 eggs**
2 tablespoons chopped bell pepper	**1/4 cup shredded Cheddar cheese (1 oz.)**

Combine butter or margarine, onion, bell pepper and chiles in a 9-inch glass pie plate. Cover with waxed paper; microwave on 100% (high) 2 minutes. Spoon vegetables into another dish.

Beat eggs together in pie plate; microwave on 100% (high) 1-1/2 minutes, pushing cooked eggs toward center of dish every 30 seconds and allowing uncooked egg to flow to edge of dish. Add cooked vegetables and cheese; using a spatula, carefully lift egg layer from one side of pie plate and fold in half. Microwave on 100% (high) 1 minute, turning omelet over after 30 seconds. Eggs are done when they are almost set but are still soft. Let stand 1 minute. Season to taste. Serve immediately.

Huevos en Micro-onda

Microwave Eggs

Here is a quick way to prepare an egg for enchiladas.

Power level: high, medium-high
Cooking time: 1-1/2 to 2 minutes
Servings: 1

**1 tablespoon butter or margarine
1 egg**

Put butter or margarine in a small shallow bowl; microwave on 100% (high) 40 seconds or until melted. Break egg into melted butter or margarine; pierce yolk with a wooden pick. Cover with waxed paper; microwave on 70% (medium-high) 1 minute. Let stand 1 minute before serving. Egg will continue to cook while standing. Season to taste. Serve hot.

Tip

Do not attempt to cook an egg in its shell in the microwave oven. Pressure will build up inside the shell, causing the egg to explode. As a result, you'll have a terrible mess to clean up in your microwave oven.

The egg yolk cooks faster than the white in a microwave oven. Therefore, the egg yolk should be pricked with a toothpick or fork before microwaving. If the egg yolk is not pricked prior to cooking, the egg yolk may explode, creating a mess in your microwave oven.

Huevos con Chorizo

Eggs with Mexican Sausage

A great dish for breakfast; it's delicious served in a warm rolled flour tortilla.

Power level: high
Cooking time: 6 to 8 minutes
Servings: 4

1/2 lb. Chorizo, page 81, or 1/2 lb. commercial chorizo
2 tablespoons chopped onion
4 eggs

Crumble chorizo into a 9-inch glass pie plate; add onion. Cover with waxed paper; microwave on 100% (high) 3 to 4 minutes, stirring after 1-1/2 minutes. Meat should be completely cooked; drain off fat.

Break eggs into cooked chorizo mixture; stir until blended. Cover with waxed paper; microwave on 100% (high) 3 to 4 minutes, stirring mixture from outside to center after 2 minutes. Eggs are done when they are almost set but are still soft. Let stand 1 minute. Season to taste. Serve immediately.

Huevos Revueltos con Chile Verde

Green Chile Scrambled Eggs

Three simple ingredients turn into a wonderful dish.

Power level: high
Cooking time: 3-1/2 minutes
Servings: 2

2 tablespoons butter or margarine
2 eggs, beaten
1/4 cup chopped green chiles

Place butter or margarine in a 9-inch glass pie plate. Cover with waxed paper; microwave on 100% (high) 1-1/2 minutes or until melted. Stir in eggs and chiles. Cover with waxed paper; microwave on 100% (high) 2 minutes, stirring from outside to center after 1 minute. Eggs are done when they are almost set but are still soft. Let stand 1 minute. Season to taste. Serve immediately.

Tortilla de Huevo

Flat Mexican Omelet

My version of the basic Mexican omelet.

Power level: high
Cooking time: 5 minutes
Servings: 4

1 tablespoon butter or margarine	2 tablespoons chopped onion
3 eggs	2 tablespoons chopped bell pepper
1/2 cup shredded Cheddar cheese (2 oz.)	2 tablespoons chopped green chiles
2 tablespoons milk	1/4 cup Taco Sauce, page 7, if desired

Place butter or margarine in a 9-inch glass pie plate; microwave on 100% (high) 40 seconds or until melted. Put eggs, 1/4 cup cheese, milk, onion, bell pepper and chiles in a separate bowl; stir to blend. Pour egg mixture into melted butter or margarine; microwave on 100% (high) 2 minutes. Push cooked egg mixture toward center of dish every 30 seconds, allowing uncooked egg to flow to edge of dish. Microwave on 100% (high) 2 minutes. Eggs are done when they are almost set but are still soft. Let stand 1 minute. Pour Taco Sauce over eggs, if desired. Top with remaining cheese. Serve immediately.

COMIDAS de ARROZ, FRIJOLES y PASTA

Beans are included in the family meal. A bowl of beans in its own liquid or Frijoles Refritos is usually served with all Mexican meals—breakfast, lunch or supper. Beans go with any food from meat to chicken, corn dishes, cheese dishes and chile dishes. Two variations, cooked fresh pinto beans and refried beans, are fast and easy to prepare.

The beans I use in my recipes are the spotted bean variety, commonly referred to as "pinto beans." Before my mother cooked beans, she would have me remove any stones, twigs, dirt or any bad-looking beans. I would then wash the beans and soak them in water for the next day's cooking.

In my family, beans were prepared at the beginning of the week and served as fresh beans in their liquid. After two or three days, my mother would mash the beans and then fry them in a skillet of hot lard or oil, at which time we referred to them as "frijoles refritos" or refried beans.

Arroz Español

Spanish Rice

Serve this very traditional tasty rice with any Mexican dish.

Power level: high
Cooking time: 21 minutes
Servings: 6

1 (10-oz.) pkg. frozen peas and carrots
3 tablespoons vegetable oil
1/4 cup chopped onion
1 garlic clove, mashed
1/4 cup chopped bell pepper

2 cups uncooked quick-cooking rice
1 (14-1/2-oz.) can chicken broth
1 (8-oz.) can tomato sauce
1/2 teaspoon salt
1/2 teaspoon dried leaf oregano, crushed

Place peas and carrots in a 1-1/2-quart casserole; cover and microwave on 100% (high)
9 minutes. Drain off liquid. Place peas and carrots in another dish; set aside.

Combine oil, onion, garlic and bell pepper in first casserole. Cover with waxed paper;
microwave on 100% (high) 2 minutes. Stir in rice, cooked peas and carrots, broth, tomato
sauce, salt and oregano. Cover and microwave on 100% (high) 10 minutes. Let stand
5 minutes before serving.

I have always thought that the addition of peas and carrots gives Spanish Rice a pretty color. Traditionally, the rice is a long-grain variety and is browned in fat with onion and garlic before adding water. I find that using instant rice and chicken broth enhances the taste and speeds up the cooking.

Sopa de Fideos

Vermicelli

"Sopa seca" or dry soup, is pasta cooked in a broth until the liquid is absorbed.

Power level: high
Cooking time: 13 minutes
Servings: 6

1/4 cup chopped bell pepper
2 tomatoes, blanched, page 4, or 1 cup
  canned tomatoes
1/4 cup chopped onion
1 garlic clove, chopped

2 tablespoons bacon drippings or
  vegetable shortening
4 oz. coiled vermicelli (2-1/2 cups)
2-1/2 cups chicken broth or beef broth
1/2 teaspoon salt, if desired

Combine bell pepper, tomatoes, onion, garlic and bacon drippings or shortening in a 2-quart casserole. Cover with waxed paper; microwave on 100% (high) 3 minutes. Break vermicelli into pieces; stir vermicelli, broth and salt, if desired, into tomato mixture. If broth is salty, omit salt. Cover with waxed paper; microwave on 100% (high) 10 minutes, stirring after 5 minutes. Let stand 5 minutes before serving. Vermicelli should be tender but firm when done.

As a child, I enjoyed my mother's Sopa de Fideos. I usually had sopa with a quesadilla as a light lunch. My recipe is an adaptation of my mother's. It is delicious and easy to prepare. Try pouring your favorite meat sauce over the sopa.

Frijoles

Pinto Beans

Pinto beans are easy to prepare. It is best to soak beans overnight before cooking.

Power level: high
Cooking time: 45 minutes to 1 hour
Servings: 4 to 5 cups

2 cups pinto beans
6 cups water
1 garlic clove
2 teaspoons salt

For conventional microwave method, soak beans in water overnight. Combine soaked beans and soaking water with garlic in a 3-quart glass bowl. Cover with waxed paper; microwave on 100% (high) 50 minutes. Let beans stand 5 minutes. Stir in salt. If beans are not fully cooked, cover and microwave on 100% (high) another 5 to 10 minutes or until tender. Serve hot.

For a microwave pressure cooker, reduce pinto beans to 1-1/2 cups and salt to 1 teaspoon. Soak beans in 6 cups water overnight. Combine soaked beans and soaking water with garlic in a microwave pressure cooker. Close pressure cooker; put on pressure-regulator weight. Microwave on 100% (high) 45 minutes. Let pressure cooker stand with pressure 10 minutes. If pressure cooker has a pressure-indicating gauge or stem, allow standing time to be the time it takes for indicator to show pressure has dropped. Remove pressure-regulator weight; open pressure cooker. Stir in salt. Beans are ready to serve.

Frijoles Refritos

Refried Beans

Don't know what to do with extra cooked pinto beans? Try refried beans.

Power level: high
Cooking time: 5 minutes
Servings: 2 cups

1 tablespoon bacon drippings or
**   vegetable shortening**
1 garlic clove, mashed
1/8 teaspoon whole cominos, crushed

1/8 teaspoon dried leaf oregano, crushed
2 cups cooked Pinto Beans, mashed, page
**   68, or 1 (16-oz.) can refried beans**
3/4 cup shredded Cheddar cheese (3 oz.)

Combine bacon drippings or shortening, garlic, cominos and oregano in a large casserole. Cover with waxed paper; microwave on 100% (high) 2 minutes. Stir in beans and 1/2 cup cheese. Cover with waxed paper; microwave on 100% (high) 3 minutes. Sprinkle with remaining cheese. Serve immediately.

Arroz Verde

Green Rice

Bell pepper, fresh cilantro and serrano or jalapeño chiles give this dish a pleasing taste and its attractive green color.

Power level: high
Cooking time: 10 minutes
Servings: 5 to 6

2 tablespoons vegetable oil
1/4 cup chopped onion
1 garlic clove, chopped
1/4 cup chopped bell pepper
1 fresh serrano or jalapeño chile, finely
    chopped, if desired

2 cups uncooked quick-cooking rice
2 cups chicken broth or 2 chicken bouil-
    lon cubes dissolved in 2 cups hot water
1/2 teaspoon salt
1/4 cup chopped fresh cilantro or parsley

Combine oil, onion, garlic, bell pepper and chile, if desired, in a 2-quart casserole. Cover with waxed paper; microwave on 100% (high) 2 minutes. Stir rice, broth, salt and cilantro or parsley into onion mixture. Cover with waxed paper; microwave on 100% (high) 8 minutes. Let stand 5 minutes before serving.

COMIDAS de CARNE

Shredding cooked beef or pork is a popular method of preparing meat dishes. Shredded meats are simmered in an array of sauces. Two favorites that use shredded meat are Machaca and Carne Adobada.

I enjoy preparing a "caldo" or soup with my meals. Caldos contain a variety of spices and are very flavorful. They are generally made with stock, either chicken or beef. To save time in my soup preparations, I substitute beef or chicken bouillon cubes or use chicken consomme or beef broth in place of preparing stock.

"Sopa aguada" or wet soup, is a vegetable or meat soup made with broth. Caldo de Cocido, boiled-meat soup, is a clear soup made with meat and vegetables.

Sopas, which include such soups as Posole or Albóndigas, are vegetable or meat soups with a flour or corn thickening base. These soups are regarded as a complete meal. "Cal-dillo" or Mexican Stew, also a sopa, is a great dish for a cold winter days. Diced potatoes add to the meal. Potatoes are used as a filler in many Mexican dishes, such as meat burritos, tacos, chorizo or scrambled eggs.

The sound of sizzling meat and the aroma of a barbecue on an outside open fire concluded many weekend family-and-friend-get-togethers. Not only were there backyard gatherings, but it was an exciting event to meet along the banks of the Rio Grande for an open-pit barbecue.

Today when I barbecue outside on an open fire, I find that partially cooking the meat in the microwave oven beforehand shortens the barbecuing time. I place the meat in a covered casserole dish and microwave on 50% (medium) power until the meat is about half-cooked. I then take the meat outside and complete the barbecue— with Chile Barbecue Sauce of course!

Albóndigas

Meatball Soup

Mint leaves give this main-dish soup a very distinctive flavor.

Power level: high, medium-high
Cooking time: 22 minutes
Servings: 4

1 lb. ground beef
3 tablespoons Taco Seasoning Mix, page
    7, or 1 (1-1/4-oz.) pkg. taco seasoning
    mix
1/2 cup dry bread crumbs
1 egg

4 cups beef broth or 4 beef bouillon
    cubes dissolved in 4 cups hot water
2 tablespoons all-purpose flour
2 teaspoons dried mint leaves
1/2 teaspoon salt
1 teaspoon azafrán, if desired

Combine ground beef, seasoning mix, bread crumbs and egg in a bowl. Shape mixture into 24 meatballs. Place meatballs in a microwave browning dish or 2-quart casserole. Cover with waxed paper; microwave on 100% (high) 3 minutes. Rearrange meatballs; cover and microwave on 100% (high) another 3 minutes or until cooked through. Drain off fat; set meatballs aside.

Combine broth and flour in a 2-quart casserole; beat with a whisk until smooth. Cover with waxed paper; microwave on 100% (high) 6 minutes or until boiling.

Drop cooked meatballs into hot broth along with mint, salt and azafrán, if desired. Cover and microwave on 70% (medium-high) 10 minutes, stirring after 5 minutes. Serve hot.

Tip

Fresh mint leaves can be dried in a microwave. Remove leaves from stems; scatter about 1/4 cup leaves on a paper napkin. Microwave on 100% (high) 1 to 2 minutes or until dried. Store in an airtight container.

Barbacoa de Costillas

Chile Barbecued Ribs

If you enjoy the great taste of barbecue, you will love this spicy sauce and ribs.

Power level: medium or high
Cooking time: 70 minutes,
   or 25 minutes in microwave pressure cooker
Servings: 4

3 lbs. pork or beef spareribs
1 cup Chile Barbecue Sauce, page 13

If using an open dish, separate individual spareribs. Place ribs, meaty side up, in a 12" x 8" flat-bottom casserole. Cover with waxed paper; microwave on 50% (medium) 40 minutes, rearranging ribs every 10 minutes. Drain off fat. Pour sauce over ribs. Cover with waxed paper; microwave on 50% (medium) 30 minutes, rearranging ribs every 10 minutes. Let stand 5 minutes before serving.

For a microwave pressure cooker, place individual ribs in pressure cooker. Add 1/4 cup water. Close pressure cooker; put on pressure-regulator weight. Microwave on 100% (high) 10 minutes. Let pressure cooker stand with pressure 5 minutes. If pressure cooker has a pressure-indicating gauge or stem, allow standing time to be the time it takes for indicator to show pressure has dropped. Remove pressure-regulator weight; open pressure cooker. Drain off and discard liquid from ribs. Pour barbecue sauce over ribs. To keep ribs from over-browning, place foil over ribs as described for covering tamales, page 32, if desired.

Close pressure cooker; put on pressure-regulator weight. Microwave on 100% (high) 15 minutes. Let pressure cooker stand with pressure 10 minutes. If pressure cooker has a pressure-indicating gauge or stem, allow standing time to be the time it takes for indicator to show pressure has dropped. Remove pressure-regulator weight; open pressure cooker. Serve ribs hot.

Caldillo

Mexican Stew

A delicious, thick, hearty stew; great served with warm tortillas.

Power level: medium, medium-high, high
Cooking time: 27 to 33 minutes
Servings: 4

**1 lb. lean beef round steak, cut in 1-inch
    cubes**
1/2 cup water
1 garlic clove, chopped
1/2 cup chopped onion
1/2 teaspoon whole cominos, crushed

1/2 teaspoon dried leaf oregano, crushed
2 cups diced potatoes
1/4 cup diced green chiles
1/2 teaspoon salt
1/2 cup water
1-1/2 tablespoons all-purpose flour

If using a covered dish, combine beef, 1/2 cup water, garlic, onion, cominos and oregano in a 2-quart casserole. Cover with a lid; microwave on 50% (medium) 10 minutes. Add potatoes, chiles and salt. Cover and microwave on 70% (medium-high) 15 to 20 minutes, stirring after 8 minutes.

Combine 1/2 cup water and flour in a small bowl, stirring until smooth. Stir into meat mixture. Cover and microwave on 100% (high) 2 to 3 minutes or until tender; stir mixture. Let stand 5 minutes before serving.

Caldo de Cocido

Boiled Meat Soup

Have your butcher cut the beef short ribs in half.

Power level: high, medium, medium-high
Cooking time: 58 to 63 minutes
Servings: 4 to 6

1 cup uncooked quick-cooking rice	1/2 teaspoon dried leaf oregano
1 cup water	5 cups water
1/2 teaspoon salt	1/4 cup chopped green chiles
2-1/2 lbs. beef short ribs, cut in half	4 medium carrots, thinly sliced
1/4 cup chopped onion	2 cups thinly sliced zucchini
1/4 cup chopped bell pepper	1 teaspoon salt
1 garlic clove, chopped	1 tablespoon chopped fresh cilantro

Combine rice, 1 cup water and 1/2 teaspoon salt in a 1-1/2-quart casserole. Cover and microwave on 100% (high) 8 minutes or until rice is tender; set rice aside.

If using a covered dish, place short ribs, onion, bell pepper, garlic and oregano in a 3-quart casserole. Cover with a lid; microwave on 50% (medium) 20 minutes. Add 5 cups water, chiles, carrots, zucchini and 1 teaspoon salt. Cover and microwave on 70% (medium-high) 30 to 35 minutes or until tender, stirring after 15 minutes. Stir in cooked rice; garnish with cilantro. Serve hot.

If using an oven-cooking bag, follow method for preparing and using a cooking bag, page 33. Place short ribs, onion, bell pepper, garlic, oregano and 1/4 cup water in cooking bag. Place bag in a 3-quart casserole. Microwave on 50% (medium) 20 minutes, turning bag over after 10 minutes.

Pour contents of cooking bag into 3-quart casserole. Add 5 cups water, chiles, carrots, zucchini and 1 teaspoon salt. Cover and microwave on 70% (medium-high) 30 to 35 minutes or until tender, stirring after 15 minutes. Add rice; garnish with cilantro. Serve hot.

Caldo de Cocido #2

This version uses the microwave pressure cooker.

Power level: high
Cooking time: 25 minutes
Servings: 4 to 5

1 cup uncooked quick-cooking rice	1/2 teaspoon dried leaf oregano
1 cup water	1/4 cup chopped green chiles
1/2 teaspoon salt	2-1/2 cups water
1-1/2 lbs. beef short ribs, cut in half	2 medium carrots, thinly sliced
1/4 cup chopped onion	1 cup thinly sliced zucchini
1/4 cup chopped bell pepper	1 teaspoon salt
1 garlic clove, minced	1 tablespoon chopped fresh cilantro

Combine rice, 1 cup water and 1/2 teaspoon salt in a 1-1/2-quart casserole. Cover and microwave on 100% (high) 8 minutes or until rice is tender: set rice aside.

Place short ribs, onion, bell pepper, garlic, oregano, chiles, 2-1/2 cups water, carrots and zucchini in a microwave pressure cooker. Close pressure cooker; put on pressure-regulator weight. Microwave on 100% (high) 25 minutes. Let pressure cooker stand with pressure 10 minutes. If pressure cooker has a pressure-indicating gauge or stem, allow standing time to be the time it takes for indicator to show pressure has dropped. Remove pressure-regulator weight; open pressure cooker. Stir in cooked rice and salt; garnish with cilantro. Serve hot.

Carne Adobada

Marinated Meat

Adobada is a thick sauce made with red chile sauce, vinegar and spices. Meat was prepared in this manner as a means of preserving it. Serve this tasty combination rolled inside warm tortillas.

Power level: medium
Cooking time: 50 minutes
Servings: 5

2 lbs. sliced pork roast, about 1/2-inch
    thick
2 cups cooked Chile Colorado, page 8
1/4 cup vinegar

2 tablespoons vegetable oil
1 garlic clove, chopped
3 whole cloves

If using a covered dish, place sliced pork in a large, flat-bottom casserole. Combine Chile Colorado, vinegar, oil, garlic and cloves in a separate dish; pour mixture over pork slices. Cover and refrigerate overnight.

Remove whole cloves from pork. Cover with a lid; microwave on 50% (medium) 50 minutes, rearranging meat every 10 minutes. Pork should be tender. If not, cover and microwave on 50% (medium) another 10 minutes. Let stand 5 minutes before serving.

If using an oven-cooking bag, marinate pork as described above. Follow method for preparing and using a cooking bag, page 33. Remove whole cloves from pork. Place marinated pork and sauce in cooking bag. Place bag in a flat-bottom casserole. Microwave on 50% (medium) 50 minutes or until tender, turning bag over after 25 minutes. Serve hot.

Carne con Chile Colorado

Red Chile Meat

Simmering the meat in the red chile sauce will enhance the flavor of this dish.

Power level: medium, medium-high
Cooking time: 30 to 35 minutes
Servings: 4 to 5

1 lb. lean pork or beef, cut in 1-inch cubes	1/2 teaspoon salt
1 garlic clove, mashed	2 cups uncooked Chile Colorado,
1/8 teaspoon whole cominos, crushed	page 8
1/8 teaspoon cilantro seeds, crushed	1 tablespoon all-purpose flour
1/8 teaspoon dried leaf oregano, crushed	

If using a covered dish, place meat in a 1-1/2-quart casserole. Cover with a lid; microwave on 50% (medium) 15 minutes. Stir in garlic, cominos, cilantro, oregano and salt; set mixture aside.

Combine Chile Colorado and flour in a small bowl; pour mixture over meat mixture. Cover with a lid or waxed paper; microwave on 70% (medium-high) 20 minutes or until tender, stirring after 10 minutes. Serve hot.

If using an oven-cooking bag, follow method for preparing and using a cooking bag, page 33. Place meat in cooking bag. Add garlic, cominos, cilantro, oregano, salt and Chile Colorado. Shake bag gently to combine ingredients. Place bag in a 1-1/2-quart casserole. Microwave on 70% (medium-high) 30 minutes, turning bag over after 15 minutes. Meat should be tender. If not, microwave on 70% (medium-high) 5 minutes or until tender. Serve hot.

Carne con Verduras (Photo front cover)

Vegetables with Meat

Spicy seasonings are added to these vegetables and meat to give this dish a zesty flavor. A great dish to serve with steamy rice.

Power level: medium, medium-high
Cooking time: 30 to 35 minutes
Servings: 4

1 lb. beef round steak, cut in 1-inch cubes
1/2 cup water
1/3 cup chopped onion
1/3 cup chopped bell pepper
1 cup diced zucchini
1 (10-oz.) pkg. frozen whole-kernel corn

1 tomato, chopped
1/4 cup diced green chiles
1 garlic clove, chopped
1/2 teaspoon dried leaf oregano, crushed
1/2 teaspoon salt

If using a covered dish, combine beef and water in a 2-quart casserole. Cover with lid; microwave on 50% (medium) 10 minutes. Add remaining ingredients; cover and microwave on 70% (medium-high) 20 to 25 minutes or until tender, stirring after 10 minutes. Serve hot.

If using an oven-cooking bag, follow method for preparing and using a cooking bag, page 33. Combine beef and water in cooking bag. Shake bag gently to combine. Place bag in a 2-quart casserole. Microwave on 50% (medium) 10 minutes. Open cooking bag; add remaining ingredients. Secure bag above vent holes; microwave on 70% (medium-high) 20 minutes or until tender, turning bag over after 10 minutes. Serve hot.

Variation

Add 2 cups of cooked pinto beans and 2 chopped green onions during final cooking period.

Chile con Carne (Photo back cover)

Chile with Meat

Serve this favorite with warm flour tortillas.

Power level: high, medium, medium-high
Cooking time: 38 minutes
Servings: 6

1/2 cup chopped onion
1/2 cup chopped bell pepper
1 garlic clove, chopped
2 tablespoons vegetable oil
1 lb. beef sirloin or top round, cut in 1-
   inch cubes
2 cups Stewed Tomatoes, page 4, or
   1 (16-oz.) can stewed tomatoes
2 cups cooked Pinto Beans, drained, page
   68, or 2 (15-oz.) cans pinto beans

3 tablespoons red chile powder
2 tablespoons all-purpose flour
1 teaspoon salt
1/4 teaspoon whole cominos, crushed
1/4 teaspoon dried leaf oregano, crushed
1 cup shredded lettuce, if desired
1 cup shredded Cheddar cheese (4 oz.), if
   desired

Combine onion, bell pepper, garlic and oil in a 1-1/2-quart casserole. Cover with waxed paper; microwave on 100% (high) 3 minutes. Set aside.

Place beef in a 2-1/2-quart casserole. Cover and microwave on 50% (medium) 10 minutes. Drain beef, reserving drippings. Add 1/2 cup beef drippings, cooked vegetables and remaining ingredients to cooked beef; stir to combine. Cover and microwave on 70% (medium-high) 25 minutes or until tender, stirring after 12 minutes. Let stand 5 minutes before serving. Garnish with shredded lettuce and cheese, if desired. Serve hot.

Chorizo

Seasoned Sausage

Chorizo goes great with Huevos Revueltos, scrambled eggs, page 63.

Power level: high
Cooking time: 4 to 6 minutes
Servings: 5 to 6

1/4 teaspoon coriander seed
1/2 teaspoon whole cominos
1 teaspoon dried leaf oregano
3 garlic cloves
1 lb. fresh bulk pork sausage

2 tablespoons red chile powder
1 teaspoon salt
1 teaspoon paprika
3 tablespoons white vinegar

Use a molcajete, see below, or mortal and pestle to prepare spices. If unavailable, use a fork and a small plate to crush spices. Crush together coriander, cominos, oregano and garlic. Add crushed spices to sausage along with chile powder, salt and paprika. Thoroughly blend sausage and seasonings. Add vinegar; blend well. Refrigerate 24 to 48 hours before using.

Crumble chorizo in a 2-quart casserole. Cover with waxed paper; microwave on 100% (high) 4 to 6 minutes, stirring after 3 minutes. Sausage should not be pink. If additional cooking is needed, cover and microwave on 100% (high) 1 minute or until cooked. Drain off fat. Serve hot.

Tip

A *molcajete*, pronounced mohl-kah-heh-teh, and *tejolete*, pronounced te-ho-leh-teh, is a three-legged mortar and pestle made of volcanic rock. It is used for grinding spices and making chile sauces. Using this device can save time, although it is not absolutely required for grinding and mashing.

Chuletas de Puerco en Chile

Chile Pork Chops

An excellent and very easy way to prepare tasty pork chops.

Power level: medium-high
Cooking time: 24 minutes
Servings: 4

3 tablespoons Taco Seasoning Mix, page 7, or 1 (1-1/4-oz.) pkg. taco seasoning mix
3 tablespoons all-purpose flour
4 pork chops

Shake seasoning mix and flour in a plastic bag. Place each pork chop into bag, shaking to coat with mixture. Place seasoned chops in a microwave browning dish or 2-quart casserole. Cover with waxed paper; microwave on 70% (medium-high) 12 minutes. Turn chops over and rotate dish; microwave on 70% (medium-high) 12 minutes or until chops are done. Let stand 5 minutes before serving. Serve hot.

Chuletas de Puerco en Mole Verde

Pork Chops in Green-Chile Sauce

Delight friends and family with this unusual combination. The sauce gives the pork a spicy, nutty taste.

Power level: medium-high
Cooking time: 24 minutes
Servings: 4

4 pork chops
1-1/2 cups Mole Verde, page 15

Place pork chops in a flat-bottom casserole. Cover with waxed paper; microwave on 70% (medium-high) 4 minutes. Turn chops over and rotate dish. Cover with waxed paper; microwave on 70% (medium-high) 4 minutes. Drain off any fat.

Pour Mole Verde over chops. Cover with waxed paper; microwave on 70% (medium-high) 16 minutes, rotating dish after 8 minutes. Chops should be done. If not, cover and microwave on 70% (medium-high) 2 minutes or until chops are done. Serve hot.

Tip

Simmering the Mole Verde on 50% (medium) 20 minutes before pouring it over the pork chops enhances the flavor of this dish. Mole Verde can also be poured over cooked, shredded pork and served rolled in a warm tortilla.

Fajitas

Little Thin Belts

A very popular meat dish today is Fajitas, translated "little thin belts."

Power level: high, medium
Cooking time: 12 minutes
Servings: 4 to 5

1 lb. beef skirt steak, flank steak or top round steak	1 tablespoon lemon juice
1/2 teaspoon whole cominos, crushed	1 teaspoon onion powder
1/4 teaspoon dried leaf oregano, crushed	1 teaspoon garlic powder
3 garlic cloves, mashed	1-1/2 cups coarsely chopped tomatoes
1/4 cup water	1 cup coarsely chopped bell pepper
1 teaspoon white pepper	1-1/2 cups coarsely chopped onion
1 teaspoon black pepper	1 cup coarsely chopped bell pepper
1 teaspoon paprika	2 tablespoons vegetable oil

Using a meat mallet, pound both sides of meat several times to tenderize. Slice beef across grain in 1/4-inch-thick lengthwise strips. Combine all ingredients except oil in a large bowl. Marinate steak strips and vegetables at least 1 hour, turning beef and vegetables after 30 minutes. Meat and vegetables can be marinated for longer periods for greater flavor enhancement.

Heat a microwave browning dish at 100% (high) 4 minutes. Use hot pads to remove dish from oven. Drain meat strips, reserving marinade. Place half the meat strips in hot browning dish. Cover with waxed paper; microwave on 50% (medium) 4 to 5 minutes, rearranging strips after 2 minutes. Repeat with remaining meat strips. Set meat aside.

Place 2 tablespoons oil in a 2-quart casserole; add vegetables to oil. Cover with waxed paper; microwave on 100% (high) 4 minutes, stirring after 2 minutes. Add meat strips and salt. Serve hot.

Fajitas have been a traditional Mexican food in the cattle country along the Mexican border. These marinated steak strips are traditionally eaten rolled in a warm flour tortilla, topped with salsa, shredded cheese and shredded lettuce.

I suppose you can say that Fajitas are a rebirth of an old idea. Originally, they were made from the tough beef skirt steak which was tenderized by pounding and marinating the beef strips in lemon or lime juice with spices added.

My mother recalls her grandmother telling her that when she worked on a ranch near the Organ Mountains in Southern New Mexico, she prepared meals in the bunk house. Every piece of meat was used including the skirt steak. She would "guisar" or stir-fry the marinated meat. She usually prepared the meat in an "olla" or large cast-iron pot, which was often too heavy for her to lift. Ranch hands would have to lift the pot for her.

Blue baked-enamel cookware was often used in place of the cast-iron because it was lighter and less expensive. I remember the neighborhood women buying it from my great-aunt Lupe's store. She always had a variety of baked-enamel cookware.

In preparing a browning dish for Fajitas, follow manufacturer's directions for heating. Although I recommend heating a browning dish 4 minutes before placing the tenderized meat strips in it, you should not heat the dish longer than recommended by the manufacturer. My recipe for Fajitas is easy to prepare and I recommend you try it!

Machaca

Shredded Beef

Machaca is an excellent filling for burritos or flautas. It is also delicious when added to frijoles.

Power level: medium, medium-high
Cooking time: 50 to 77 minutes
Servings: 6 to 8

2-1/2 lbs. boneless beef
1/4 teaspoon whole black peppercorns,
    crushed
1/4 teaspoon cilantro seed, crushed
2 garlic cloves, mashed
1/2 cup sliced onion
1/2 cup water

1/4 teaspoon whole cominos, crushed
1/2 teaspoon dried leaf oregano, crushed
1/2 teaspoon salt
1/4 cup diced green chiles
1 cup chopped Stewed Tomatoes, page 4,
    or 1 (8-oz.) can stewed tomatoes

If using a covered dish, rub beef with peppercorns, cilantro and garlic; place in a 2-quart casserole. Add onion and water. Cover with a lid; microwave on 50% (medium) 25 minutes per pound. Meat is done when it is no longer pink. If not done, cover and microwave on 50% (medium) 5 to 10 minutes or until done. Place beef on a cutting board. Reserve drippings; set aside.

When beef is cooled, shred it by pulling it apart with a fork or cut meat into strips. Place meat, cominos, oregano, salt, chiles, tomatoes and 2/3 cup reserved drippings in 2-quart casserole. Cover and microwave on 70% (medium-high) 15 minutes, stirring after 7-1/2 minutes. Season to taste.

If using an oven-cooking bag, follow method for preparing and using a cooking bag, page 33. Rub beef with peppercorns, cilantro and garlic. Place beef in cooking bag. Add onion and water. Put bag in a 2-quart casserole. Microwave on 50% (medium) 25 minutes per pound, turning bag over after 12 minutes. Open cooking bag; check meat for doneness. If not done, tie bag and microwave on 50% (medium) 5 to 10 minutes or until done. Remove beef; place on a cutting board. Reserve beef drippings; set aside. Complete as above.

Variations

Machaca #2

Microwave Pressure Cooker Method
Power level: high
Cooking time: 40 minutes
Servings: 6 to 8

Rub beef with peppercorns, cilantro and garlic. Place beef in microwave pressure cooker. Add onions and water. To keep meat from over-browning, place foil over meat, as described on page 32, if desired.

Close pressure cooker; put on pressure-regulator weight. Microwave on 100% (high) 30 minutes. Let pressure cooker stand with pressure 10 minutes. If pressure cooker has a pressure-indicating gauge or stem, allow standing time to be the time it takes for indicator to show pressure has dropped. Remove pressure-regulator weight; open pressure cooker. Remove beef; place on a cutting board. Reserve 2/3 cup beef drippings.

When beef is cooled, shred beef by pulling it apart with a fork or cut meat into strips. Add meat, cominos, oregano, salt, chiles and tomatoes to reserved drippings in pressure cooker. Place foil back over beef, if desired. Close pressure cooker; put on pressure regulator weight. Microwave on 100% (high) 10 minutes. Let pressure cooker stand with pressure 5 minutes. If pressure cooker has a pressure indicating gauge or stem, allow standing time to be the time it takes for indicator to show pressure has dropped. Remove pressure regulator weight; open pressure cooker. Serve hot.

Machaca con Chile Colorado

Shredded Beef with Red Chili

Prepare as above, substituting 2 cups cooked Chile Colorado, page 8, for green chiles and omit stewed tomatoes.

Diablitas

Little She-Devils

A recipe given to me by my mother. Red chile sauce poured over spicy meatballs describes the appearance and taste of this food. But why "She-Devils" you may ask?

Power level: high, medium-high
Cooking time: 22 minutes
Servings: 4

1 lb. ground pork	**1/2 teaspoon dried leaf oregano, crushed**
1 garlic clove, chopped	**1 egg**
1/2 cup chopped onion	**2 cups cooked Chile Colorado, page 8**
1 teaspoon salt	
1/2 teaspoon whole cominos, crushed	

Combine pork, garlic, onion, salt, cominos, oregano and egg in a large bowl. Shape pork mixture into 24 meatballs, placing meatballs in a microwave browning dish or flat-bottom casserole. Cover with waxed paper; microwave on 100% (high) 4 minutes.

Rearrange meatballs by placing those that were on the outer edge of the dish in the center and those from the center around the edge. Cover and microwave on 100% (high) 4 minutes. Drain off fat; place cooked meatballs in a 2-quart casserole.

Pour Chile Colorado over meatballs. Cover and microwave on 70% (medium-high) 14 minutes, stirring after 7 minutes. Serve hot.

Posole

Meat & Hominy Soup

A wonderful dish for Christmas Eve or any cold night.

Power level: high, medium-high
Cooking time: 30 minutes
Servings: 6

2 cups diced cooked beef or pork
1 (1-lb.,13-oz.) can white hominy, drained
4 cups water
2 cups cooked Chile Colorado, page 8

1 teaspoon salt
1 teaspoon dried leaf oregano, crushed
Chopped onions, if desired
Crushed oregano, if desired

Combine beef or pork, hominy, water, Chile Colorado, salt and oregano in a deep, 3-quart casserole. Cover with waxed paper; microwave on 100% (high) 20 minutes or until mixture begins to boil. Stir well; cover and microwave on 70% (medium-high) 10 minutes, stirring after 5 minutes. Pour soup into serving bowls. Sprinkle with onions and oregano, if desired.

Tip

If time permits, simmering at a lower power level enhances the flavor of this dish.

As a child, I remember going with my father to the local Mexican restaurant with an "olla" or large pot in hand to get menudo on Saturday afternoons. It was a local custom for the neighborhood to buy their menudo from the restaurant. We would join their company with filled ollas in hand. On the way home, we would stop at the "panadería" (bakery) to buy our panecitos or little loaves to eat with menudo. Menudo is a red chile soup made with hominy and tripe. Instead of a menudo recipe, I have included a recipe for posole. Both are similar soups; menudo is made with tripe and posole is made with beef or pork.

Torta de Carne Molida

Chile Meatloaf

Meatloaf becomes a special treat served hot or cold.

Power level: medium-high
Cooking time: 20 minutes
Servings: 6

1 (8-oz.) can tomato sauce
1-1/2 lbs. ground beef
1 cup fresh bread crumbs
1/4 cup chopped onion
1/4 cup chopped bell pepper
1 garlic clove, chopped

1 egg
3 tablespoons Taco Seasoning Mix, page
   7, or 1 (1-1/4-oz.) pkg. taco seasoning mix
1/4 cup diced green chiles

Set half the tomato sauce aside. In a large bowl, combine remaining tomato sauce and all other ingredients; blend well.

Grease a microwave-safe ring mold or a round, glass cake dish. Place an inverted custard cup in center of cake dish. Pat meat mixture into greased mold or dish. Pour remaining tomato sauce over top of meat mixture.

Cover with waxed paper; microwave on 70% (medium-high) 20 minutes, rotating dish after 10 minutes. Let stand 5 minutes. If meat is still pink, cover and microwave on 70% (medium-high) 1 minute or until cooked through. Serve hot.

COMIDAS de POLLO y PESCADO

Many of my chicken dishes use a mole or pipián sauce made from blended nuts, with their origin from Mexican history.

I find that baking a whole chicken in the microwave, then boning it and freezing it in 2-cup portions works great. You always have chicken available for those "What can I prepare?" days. Recipes which use cooked chicken are tacos, enchiladas and various casseroles.

Some of my soup recipes contain chicken. Caldo de Pollo is a chicken soup containing vegetables and rice. Caldo Azteca is a chicken broth soup with pieces of chicken. Caldo de Queso is a delicious creamy soup made with chicken broth, milk and cheese.

Although there are a variety of fish dishes in the Mexican cuisine, most are identified with the coastal areas of Mexico. My recipes are based on the local supply of fish that has traditionally been available.

I remember that my mother always made it a point to use only fresh thin fillets of fish without the "espinas" or bones, because like most kids, we did not like to be bothered with bones.

Azafrán is a plentiful spice, used in cooking rice, fish and soups. The spice is made from deep-crimson pistils of the Mexican saffron crocus. Note this is a different crocus than that used for the true Turkish saffron. Azafrán gives the dish an attractive crimson-flecked color and distinctive taste.

Arroz con Pollo

Chicken with Rice

The browning mix, along with the azafrán, gives this popular dish great taste and eye appeal.

Power level: high, medium-high
Cooking time: 35 to 50 minutes
Servings: 6

Browning Mix

1 teaspoon paprika
2 tablespoons brown sugar
1/2 teaspoon poultry seasoning

1/4 teaspoon garlic salt or regular salt
1/2 teaspoon onion powder

Chicken

1 (10-oz.) pkg frozen peas and carrots, if
    desired
1 (3-1/2-lb.) frying chicken, cut into pieces
2 tablespoons vegetable oil
1/2 cup chopped onion
1/2 cup chopped bell pepper

1 garlic clove
2 cups uncooked quick-cooking rice
1/2 teaspoon salt
1 cup Stewed Tomatoes, page 4, or 1
    (8-oz.) can stewed tomatoes
1-1/2 teaspoons azafrán, if desired

For browning mix, combine all ingredients. Mixture can be made ahead and stored in an airtight container for future use.

If using peas and carrots, place in a 1-1/2-quart casserole. Cover with waxed paper; microwave on 100% (high) 10 minutes. Set vegetables aside.

Coat chicken pieces with browning mix; place coated pieces in a 2-1/2-quart casserole. Cover with waxed paper; microwave on 100% (high) 20 to 25 minutes or until cooked through, rearranging chicken pieces after 12 minutes. Pour chicken drippings into a measuring cup; set aside. Remove cooked chicken; set aside.

Combine oil, onion, bell pepper and garlic in same casserole used to cook chicken. Cover with waxed paper; microwave on 100% (high) 3 minutes. Add enough water to chicken drippings to make 2 cups. Add drippings, rice, salt, tomatoes and azafrán, if desired, to onion mixture. Cover with waxed paper; microwave on 70% (medium-high) 7 minutes. Add cooked chicken and cooked peas and carrots, if desired. Cover and microwave on 70% (medium-high) 5 minutes. Serve hot.

Tip

In many traditional Mexican recipes, the rice is browned in a skillet over medium-high heat before the addition of other ingredients. One tablespoon of oil can be added prior to adding the rice if desired. Stir rice for 4 to 5 minutes until the grains are lightly browned.

Rice can be browned in your microwave oven by placing it in a 2-quart casserole dish. Add 1 tablespoon of vegetable oil to the rice and coat it thoroughly. Microwave, uncovered on 100% (high) for 2 to 3 minutes, stirring the rice every minute until it is lightly browned. Follow the recipe as given.

The same procedure for browning rice can be used for preparation of Arroz Español, page 66, and for Sopa de Fideos, page 67.

Break the vermicelli into pieces and place in a 2-quart casserole dish. Add 1/2 tablespoon of vegetable oil and microwave on 100% (high) for 2 minutes, stirring every minute until the vermicelli is lightly browned. Follow the recipe as given.

Barbacoa de Pollo

Chile Barbecued Chicken

Spicy barbecue sauce goes well with chicken.

Power level: high
Cooking time: 20 to 25 minutes
Servings: 4 to 6

**1 (3-lb.) frying chicken, cut up
1 cup Chile Barbecue Sauce, page 13**

Place chicken in a 2-1/2-quart casserole. Pour sauce over chicken. Cover with waxed paper; microwave on 100% (high) 20 to 25 minutes, turning dish and rearranging chicken every 10 minutes or until cooked through. Let stand 5 minutes before serving.

Cacerola de Pollo

Chicken Casserole

Sour cream enhances the taste of this complete meal in a casserole.

Power level: high, medium-high
Cooking time: 14 to 16 minutes
Servings: 6

2 tablespoons vegetable oil
1/4 cup chopped bell pepper
1/2 cup chopped onion
1 garlic clove, chopped
1/8 teaspoon whole cominos, crushed
1/4 cup chopped green chiles
1 (10-1/2-oz.) can cream of chicken soup
1 cup dairy sour cream

2 eggs
2 cups diced cooked chicken
1 (11-oz.) pkg. corn chips or tortilla chips
1-1/2 cups shredded Cheddar cheese
  (6 oz.)
1/2 cup sliced ripe olives or 1 (2-1/4-oz.)
  can sliced ripe olives

Combine oil, bell pepper, onion, garlic and cominos in a 1-1/2-quart casserole. Cover with waxed paper; microwave on 100% (high) 2 minutes. Add chiles, soup and sour cream. Cover with waxed paper; microwave on 100% (high) 2 minutes. Beat eggs into mixture. Stir in chicken; set mixture aside.

Grease a 2-quart casserole. Line casserole with corn or tortilla chips. Top with 1/3 of chicken mixture; sprinkle with 1/3 the cheese and olives. Repeat with two additional layers of chips, chicken mixture, cheese and olives. Cover dish with waxed paper; microwave on 70% (medium-high) 10 to 12 minutes, rotating dish after 5 minutes.

Place remaining chips around edge of dish. Let stand 5 minutes before serving.

Caldo de Pollo

Chicken Soup

Cooked rice is added at the end of the cooking, resulting in a clear broth.

Power level: high
Cooking time: 48 minutes, or
   33 minutes for a microwave pressure cooker
Servings: 4 to 6

1 cup uncooked quick-cooking rice	1/4 cup chopped bell pepper
1 cup water	1/4 cup chopped celery
1/4 teaspoon salt	1 cup thinly sliced carrots
2 lbs. frying chicken pieces	1 garlic clove, cut in half
5 cups water	1 teaspoon poultry seasoning
1/4 cup chopped onion	1 teaspoon salt

Combine rice, 1 cup water and 1/4 teaspoon salt in a 1-1/2-quart casserole. Cover and microwave on 100% (high) 8 minutes or until tender; set rice aside.

Combine chicken pieces, 5 cups water, onion, bell pepper, celery, carrots, garlic, poultry seasoning and 1 teaspoon salt in a 3-quart casserole. Cover and microwave on 100% (high) 40 minutes, stirring after 20 minutes. Vegetables and chicken should be tender. Stir in cooked rice. Let stand 5 minutes before serving.

For a microwave pressure cooker, prepare rice as above; set aside. Reduce chicken to 1-1/2 pounds and use 3-1/2 cups water. Combine chicken, water, onion, bell pepper, celery, carrots, garlic, poultry seasoning and salt in a microwave pressure cooker. Close pressure cooker; put on pressure-regulator weight. Microwave on 100% (high) 25 minutes. Let pressure cooker stand with pressure 10 minutes. If pressure cooker has a pressure-indicating gauge or stem, allow standing time to be the time it takes for indicator to show pressure has dropped. Remove pressure-regulator weight; open pressure cooker. Stir in cooked rice. Let stand 5 minutes before serving.

Chile Verde con Pollo

Green Chile with Chicken

This dish is a variation of the enchilada.

Power level: high, medium-high
Cooking time: 21 minutes
Servings: 6

1/2 cup chopped onion
1/2 cup chopped bell pepper
1 garlic clove, chopped
2 tablespoons vegetable oil
1/2 cup diced green chiles
1/4 teaspoon paprika
1 cup chicken broth or 1 chicken bouillon
  cube dissolved in 1 cup hot water

1 (10-1/2-oz.) can cream of chicken soup
1/4 cup half and half
1 cup shredded Cheddar cheese (4 oz.)
12 (6-inch) corn tortillas, cut in 3/4-inch
  strips
2 cups diced cooked chicken

Combine onion, bell pepper, garlic and oil in a 2-quart casserole. Cover with waxed paper; microwave on 100% (high) 4 minutes, stirring after 2 minutes. Add chiles, paprika, broth, soup and half and half; set mixture aside.

Grease a 2-quart casserole. Set 1/4 cup cheese aside. With remaining cheese, build alternate layers of tortilla strips, chicken, cheese and chicken sauce in greased casserole. Continue alternating layers until all ingredients are used, making the last layer with chicken sauce.

Cover with waxed paper; microwave on 70% (medium-high) 15 minutes, turning dish after 7-1/2 minutes. Sprinkle reserved 1/4 cup cheese on top. Cover with waxed paper; microwave on 70% (medium-high) 2 minutes. Let stand 5 minutes before serving.

Mole de Pollo

Chicken Mole

Mole Colorado is a Mexican sauce made of an unusual combination of chile, chocolate, cinnamon and peanut butter. Simmer the sauce to enhance the flavor.

Power level: high, medium-high
Cooking time: about 1 hour
Servings: 6

1 (3-lb.) frying chicken	1 small onion, cut in half
Dash of salt	1 garlic clove, cut in half
Dash of pepper	3-1/2 cups Mole Colorado, page 14

Rinse whole chicken; season cavity with salt and pepper. Insert onion and garlic in cavity. Place seasoned chicken in a 2-quart casserole. Cover with waxed paper; microwave on 100% (high) 24 to 26 minutes, turning chicken over and rotating dish after 12 minutes. Chicken is done when flesh near bones is no longer pink. If not done, microwave on 100% (high) 5 minutes or until cooked through. Let stand 10 minutes.

Remove chicken from casserole; set aside. Pour chicken drippings into a 1-quart measure; add water to make 3 cups liquid. Set liquid aside.

Remove cooked onion and garlic from chicken cavity; discard. Bone chicken; add cooked chicken to Mole Colorado. Spoon sauce over chicken. Cover with waxed paper; microwave on 70% (medium-high) 15 minutes, stirring after 7 minutes. Serve hot.

Mole de Pollo #2

Chicken Mole

Microwave Pressure Cooker Method
Power level: high
Cooking time: 22 minutes
Servings: 6

1 (3-lb.) frying chicken	**1 small onion, cut in half**
Dash of salt	**1/4 cup water**
Dash of pepper	**3-1/2 cups Mole Colorado, page 14**

For a microwave pressure cooker, rinse whole chicken; season cavity with salt and pepper. Insert onion and garlic in cavity. Place seasoned chicken in a microwave pressure cooker; add 1/4 cup water. Close pressure cooker; put on pressure-regulator weight. Microwave on 100% (high) 22 minutes. Let pressure cooker stand with pressure 10 minutes. If pressure cooker has a pressure-indicating gauge or stem, allow standing time to be the time it takes for indicator to show pressure has dropped. Remove pressure-regulator weight; open pressure cooker.

Remove chicken; set aside. Pour chicken drippings into a 1-quart measure; add water to make 3 cups liquid. Set liquid aside. Remove onion and garlic, discard. Bone chicken.

Prepare Mole Colorado in a 2-1/2-quart casserole; add chicken and reserved 3 cups chicken liquid. Cover with waxed paper; microwave on 70% (medium-high) 20 minutes, stirring after 10 minutes.

Variation

Mole sauce also goes great over cooked turkey or pork. Water or beef broth can be substituted for 3 cups chicken broth.

Pollo Borracho

Drunken Chicken

Pollo Borracho has always been a favorite in my family. My daughter is always asking me to prepare it for her. I use cooking sherry, but you can also use flat beer.

Power level: high, medium-high
Cooking time: 41 to 46 minutes
Servings: 6

3 tablespoons butter or margarine
1/4 cup chopped onion
1 garlic clove, chopped
1/2 teaspoon dried leaf oregano, crushed
1 (8-oz.) can tomato sauce
1/4 cup water

1/2 cup cooking sherry or flat beer
3 tablespoons Taco Seasoning Mix, page 7, or 1 (1-1/4-oz.) pkg. taco seasoning mix
3 tablespoons all-purpose flour
1 (3-1/2-lb.) frying chicken, cut up

Combine butter or margarine, onion, garlic and oregano in a 2-1/2-quart casserole. Cover with waxed paper; microwave on 100% (high) 3 minutes. Stir in tomato sauce and water. Cover with waxed paper; microwave on 70% (medium-high) 5 minutes. Pour tomato mixture into a bowl. After tomato mixture cools, add sherry or beer; set aside.

Combine seasoning mix and flour in a plastic bag; add chicken pieces. Shake bag gently, coating chicken evenly with seasoning. Place seasoned chicken pieces in 2-1/2-quart casserole. Cover with waxed paper; microwave on 100% (high) 18 minutes, rearranging pieces and turning dish after 9 minutes. Pour off excess drippings. Pour tomato mixture over chicken. Cover with waxed paper; microwave on 70% (medium-high) 15 to 20 minutes or until chicken and sauce is bubbly hot. Serve immediately.

Pollo con Queso

Chicken with Cheese

Your own taco-flavored tortilla chips, page 50, will give this dish that special flavor of seasoned corn tortillas.

Power level: high
Cooking time: 12 minutes
Servings: 4

1 tablespoon butter or margarine
1/4 cup chopped onion
1/4 cup chopped bell pepper
1 (10-1/2-oz.) can cream of chicken soup
2/3 cup evaporated milk
1/4 cup diced green chiles

5 cups Seasoned Chips, page 50, or
   1 (8-oz.) bag taco-flavored corn chips
2 cups diced cooked chicken
1 cup shredded Cheddar cheese (4 oz.)
1/4 cup sliced ripe olives or 1 (2-1/4-oz.)
   can sliced ripe olives

Combine butter or margarine, onion and bell pepper in a 1-1/2-quart casserole. Cover with waxed paper; microwave on 100% (high) 2 minutes. Stir in soup, evaporated milk and chiles; set mixture aside.

Reserve 12 tortilla chips, 1/3 cup cheese and 2 tablespoons olives for topping.

Grease a 1-1/2-quart casserole. Using 1/3 of remaining tortilla chips, make a layer of chips in casserole. Top with 1/3 of soup mixture and 1/3 of chicken. Sprinkle a layer of cheese and olives over chicken. Continue layering until all ingredients are used, making the last layer chicken. Cover with waxed paper; microwave on 100% (high) 9 minutes, turning dish every 3 minutes.

Sprinkle reserved cheese and olives over top. Cover with waxed paper; microwave on 100% (high) 1 minute or until cheese melts. Stand remaining tortilla chips around edge of casserole. Serve hot.

Rellenos de Cocono

Turkey Rellenos

The mild taste of ground turkey in the Rellenos de Cocono is enhanced by the unique taste of fresh mature red chile.

Power level: high
Cooking time: 9 to 10 minutes
Servings: 3

1/2 lb. ground turkey	3 eggs, separated
1/4 teaspoon salt	1/4 teaspoon cream of tartar, if desired
1/4 teaspoon garlic powder	2 tablespoons all-purpose flour
1/2 teaspoon onion powder	1/2 teaspoon baking powder
1/2 teaspoon dried leaf oregano, crushed	1/4 teaspoon paprika
6 fresh red chiles, roasted, page 3, or	1/8 teaspoon salt
1 (8-oz.) can whole roasted or canned	1/8 teaspoon pepper
green chiles	2 tablespoons butter or margarine
1-1/2 cups shredded Monterey Jack	
cheese (6 oz.)	

Place turkey in a 2-quart casserole. Cover with waxed paper; microwave on 100% (high) 3 minutes, stirring after 1-1/2 minutes. Turkey is cooked when it is no longer pink. Let stand 5 minutes. Drain turkey, discarding liquid. Stir in salt, garlic powder, onion powder and oregano; set mixture aside.

Roast and peel fresh chiles, page 3. Remember to avoid touching face. Cut a lengthwise slit along each chile pod; remove seeds.

Reserve 3/4 cup cheese for topping. Using remaining cheese, fill each chile with 2 tablespoons turkey mixture and 1 tablespoon cheese; set stuffed chiles aside.

Beat egg whites with an electric mixer until stiff, gradually beating in 1/4 teaspoon cream of tartar to stiffen egg whites, if desired. Stir together egg yolks, flour, baking powder, paprika, salt and pepper in a separate bowl. Fold egg-yolk mixture into beaten egg-whites to make batter. Pour batter into a shallow glass pie plate; set aside.

Place butter or margarine in a 12" x 8" flat-bottom casserole. Cover with waxed paper; microwave on 100% (high) 1-1/2 minutes or until melted. Dip each stuffed chile into batter, then place in casserole. Arrange stuffed chiles side-by-side in casserole. Cover with waxed paper; microwave on 100% (high) 2 minutes. Turn chiles over with a spatula. Continue to microwave on 100% (high) 2 more minutes. Rellenos are done when batter is cooked. If batter does not appear to be cooked, microwave on 100% (high) 1 minute or until batter is cooked. Sprinkle reserved cheese over rellenos. Cover with waxed paper; microwave on 100% (high) 45 seconds or until cheese melts. Serve hot.

"Cocono" is a colloquial term for turkey that is used locally. Turkey is also referred to as "guajolote" or "pavo." Fresh red chiles are actually green chiles that have been allowed to ripen on the vine. They are seasonal and are usually available in early autumn. If you cannot find fresh red chiles, substitute whole roasted green chiles, fresh or canned.

Pollo en Pipián

Chicken in Pumpkin-Seed Sauce

Lowly pumpkin seeds add distinction to this chicken.

Power level: medium-high
Cooking time: 35 minutes
Servings: 4

1/2 cup shelled pumpkin seeds
3 cups chicken broth or 3 chicken
    bouillon cubes dissolved in 3 cups
    hot water
3 tablespoons vegetable oil
3 tablespoons all-purpose flour
1 teaspoon coriander seeds

2 tablespoons red chile powder
3 tablespoons Taco Seasoning Mix, page
    7, or 1 (1-1/4-oz.) pkg. taco season-
    ing mix
1/4 cup sesame seeds
3 cups diced cooked chicken

If pumpkin seeds are salted, rinse in water; drain well. Combine pumpkin seeds, broth, oil, flour, coriander, chile powder, seasoning mix and sesame seeds in a blender; process until liquified. Pour mixture into a 1-1/2-quart casserole. Cover with waxed paper; microwave on 70% (medium-high) 15 minutes, stirring after 7-1/2 minutes. Add chicken to hot sauce; stir to blend. Cover with waxed paper; microwave on 70% (medium-high) 20 minutes, stirring after 10 minutes. Let stand 5 minutes. Serve hot.

Caldo de Queso

Cheese Soup

Queso or cheese is added to many Mexican dishes from soups, to chiles, to vegetables and more. The combination of Monterey Jack cheese and mild Cheddar cheese makes this soup great!

Power level: high, medium-high
Cooking time: 22 minutes
Servings: 4 to 6

2 tablespoons vegetable oil
1/4 cup chopped onion
1 garlic clove, chopped
1/4 cup chopped bell pepper
1/1 teaspoon ground cominos
1/4 cup diced green chiles
1 cup chicken broth or 1 chicken bouillon
     cube dissolved in 1 cup hot water

1 tablespoon cornstarch
3 cups milk
1-1/2 cups shredded Monterey Jack
     cheese (6 oz.)
Salt to taste
1 cup shredded Cheddar cheese (4 oz.)

Combine oil, onion, garlic, bell pepper and cominos in a 2-1/2-quart casserole. Cover with waxed paper; microwave on 100% (high) 4 minutes, stirring after 2 minutes. Add chiles and broth. Cover with waxed paper; microwave on 100% (high) 10 minutes, stirring after 5 minutes.

Dissolve cornstarch in a small amount of milk; stir into chicken mixture along with remaining milk and Monterey Jack cheese. Cover with waxed paper; microwave on 70% (medium-high) 8 minutes, stirring after 4 minutes. Salt to taste. Sprinkle Cheddar cheese over top. Serve hot.

Pollo de Harina

Tortilla Chicken

Surprisingly simple to fix.

Power level: high
Cooking time: 20 to 25 minutes
Servings: 4

**1 cup cooked Chile Colorado, page 8
1/2 cup ketchup
8 chicken pieces, skinned
1 cup masa harina**

Grease a 12" x 8" flat-bottom casserole. In a small bowl, combine Chile Colorado and ketchup. Place masa harina in a pie plate. Dip each chicken piece in chile mixture; then roll in masa harina. Place coated chicken pieces in greased casserole, arranging thicker portions toward edges of dish. Pour remaining sauce over chicken.

Cover with waxed paper; microwave on 100% (high) 20 to 25 minutes, turning dish after 10 minutes. Chicken is done when flesh is no longer pink and juices run clear. Let stand 5 minutes before serving.

This is another recipe of Aztec origin, a corn-flavored chicken dish. In my recipe, ketchup is a modern substitution for sweetened tomato sauce. It saves time without sacrificing flavor. My mother handed down this simple yet delicious way to prepare chicken.

Caldo Azteca

Aztec Soup

Serve this chicken soup year 'round.

Power level: high, medium-high
Cooking time: 33 minutes
Servings: 4

2 tablespoons vegetable oil
1 garlic clove, chopped
1/2 cup chopped onion
1/2 cup chopped celery
1 cup diced cooked chicken
5 cups chicken broth or
    5 chicken bouillon cubes dissolved
    in 5 cups hot water

1/2 teaspoon poultry seasoning
3 tablespoons diced green chiles
1/2 teaspoon salt
1 cup thinly sliced carrots, if desired
3 tablespoons masa harina
1 cup water

Combine oil, garlic, onion and celery in a 2-quart casserole. Cover with waxed paper; microwave on 100% (high) 3 minutes. Stir in chicken, broth, poultry seasoning, chiles, salt and carrots, if desired. Cover with waxed paper; microwave on 100% (high) 20 minutes, stirring after 10 minutes. If using carrots, cook until tender. Set mixture aside.

Using a whisk, dissolve masa harina in 1 cup water; stir into soup mixture. Cover with waxed paper; microwave on 70% (medium-high) 10 minutes, stirring after 5 minutes. Let stand 5 minutes before serving.

My Caldo Azteca recipe has its origin in the village life of my great-grandmother when she lived in central Mexico. The term "Azteca" in the recipe name refers to the inclusion of masa harina or corn flour in the dish. This is believed to have originated from Aztec cooking, handed down to the peoples of my great-grandmother's time.

Pescado al Jardín

Garden-Style Fish

Pimiento-stuffed olives combined with seasonings create this delectable flavor.

Power level: high, medium-high
Cooking time: 16 minutes
Servings: 4 to 5

1/4 cup chopped onion	1/2 teaspoon cilantro seeds, crushed
1/4 cup chopped bell pepper	1/4 teaspoon salt
1 garlic clove, chopped	1 teaspoon dried leaf oregano, crushed
3 tablespoons olive oil	1 tablespoon lemon juice or lime juice
1/4 cup chopped pimiento-stuffed green olives	1-1/2 lbs. fish fillets
	1/2 teaspoon paprika
1/4 cup diced green chiles	2 tablespoons chopped fresh parsley

Combine onion, bell pepper, garlic and olive oil in a 12" x 8" flat-bottom casserole. Cover with waxed paper; microwave on 100% (high) 3 minutes. Add olives, chiles, cilantro, salt, oregano and lemon or lime juice; stir to combine. Cover with waxed paper; microwave on 70% (medium-high) 5 minutes. Push cooked vegetables to side of dish.

Arrange fish fillets in casserole; sprinkle with paprika. Spoon simmered vegetables over fish. Sprinkle with parsley. Cover with waxed paper; microwave on 70% (medium-high) 8 minutes, turning dish after 4 minutes. Let stand 5 minutes. Fish at center of dish should flake easily with a fork. If more cooking time is needed, cover and microwave on 70% (medium-high) 1 minute or until fish is done. Serve hot.

Tip

To dry parsley, remove coarse stems. Wash parsley thoroughly and pat dry between paper towels. Place 1 cup of parsley on a double layer of paper towels. Microwave on 100% (high) for 3 minutes, rearranging and turning parsley over every minute.

Pescado en Naranja

Fish in Orange Juice

Orange juice combined with parsley creates a unique taste for this fish.

Power level: high, medium-high
Cooking time: 11-1/2 minutes
Servings: 6

1 garlic clove, mashed	1/2 teaspoon pepper
1/4 cup butter or margarine	1-1/2 lbs. white-fish fillets
1/2 cup all-purpose flour	1/4 cup orange juice
1/2 teaspoon paprika	3 tablespoons chopped fresh parsley
1/2 teaspoon salt	1 orange, sliced, if desired

Put garlic and butter or margarine in a 12" x 8" flat-bottom casserole. Cover with waxed paper; microwave on 100% (high) 2 minutes.

In a shallow dish, combine flour, paprika, salt and pepper; coat fish fillets with flour mixture. Place each seasoned fillet in the casserole, coating both sides with garlic and melted butter. Cover with waxed paper; microwave on 100% (high) 1-1/2 minutes, turning fillets over after 45 seconds.

Pour orange juice over fish; sprinkle with parsley. Cover with waxed paper; microwave on 70% (medium-high) 8 minutes, turning dish after 4 minutes. Let stand 5 minutes. Fish at center of dish should flake easily with a fork. If more cooking time is needed, cover and microwave on 70% (medium-high) 1 minute or until done. Garnish with orange slices, if desired. Serve hot.

Pescado Empanizado

Breaded Fish

Fish is always quick to prepare in the microwave and is tender and flaky.

Power level: high
Cooking time: 8 minutes
Servings: 4

3 tablespoons bacon drippings or
   vegetable shortening
1 cup fine dry bread crumbs
1 teaspoon paprika
1/4 teaspoon dried leaf oregano, crushed

1/2 teaspoon salt
1/2 teaspoon azafrán, if desired
1/3 cup milk
1 lb. fish fillets

Put bacon drippings or shortening in a 12" x 8" flat-bottom casserole. Cover with waxed paper; microwave on 100% (high) 2 minutes.

Combine bread crumbs, paprika, oregano, salt and azafrán, if desired. Pour milk in a shallow dish. Dip each fillet in milk; then in crumb mixture. Place fillets in casserole with hot drippings or shortening. Cover with waxed paper; microwave on 100% (high) 2 minutes. Turn fillets over. Cover with waxed paper; microwave on 100% (high) 4 minutes, turning dish after 2 minutes. Let stand 5 minutes. Fish at center of dish should flake easily with a fork. If more cooking time is needed, cover and microwave on 100% (high) 1 minute or until done. Serve hot.

Pescado en Escabeche (Photo back cover)

Fish Marinated in Vinegar

If you're missing ingredients, top cooked fillets with salsa. Serve it as a main dish or appetizer.

Power level: high
Cooking time: 5 minutes
Servings: 6

3 tablespoons olive oil
1-1/2 lbs. white-fish fillets, about
   1/4-inch thick
1/2 cup chopped onion
2 garlic cloves, mashed
1/2 cup chopped bell pepper
1/4 cup diced green chile
1/2 teaspoon black pepper

1/2 cup white vinegar
1/2 teaspoon paprika
2 tablespoons lemon or lime juice
1/2 teaspoon dried leaf oregano
1/4 teaspoon cilantro seeds, crushed
1/4 cup fresh parsley or cilantro leaves
1/4 cup water

Pour oil into a 12" x 8" casserole. Place fish fillets in casserole, turning pieces to coat both sides with oil. Cover with waxed paper; microwave on 100% (high) 5 minutes, turning fish over after 2-1/2 minutes. Set fish aside.

Combine remaining ingredients in a bowl. Pour mixture over fish fillets. Cover and refrigerate fish 12 to 24 hours. Fish is ready to serve. Serve on lettuce or other greens, if desired.

Variation

Add 1-1/2 cups chopped tomatoes and 1/2 cup tomato sauce to marinating mixture. Pescado en Escabeche can also be served as an appetizer. Cut cooked, marinated fish in chunks. Serve in cocktail glasses with diced avocado and a squeeze of lime. Season to taste.

Pescado en Salsa Roja

Fish in Red Sauce

Salsa Roja is a thick red sauce that gives seafood a mild spicy taste.

Power level: high, medium-high
Cooking time: 16 minutes
Servings: 5 to 6

3 tablespoons vegetable oil
1-1/2 lbs. rock fish or red snapper fillets,
    or 1 lb. shrimp, cleaned
1 (6-oz.) can tomato paste
1 cup water
1/4 cup chopped onion

3 garlic cloves, chopped
2 tablespoons red chile powder
1/2 teaspoon dried leaf oregano
1/2 teaspoon ground cominos
1 teaspoon salt
1 lime or lemon, cut in wedges

Pour 2 tablespoons oil into a 12" x 8" casserole. Place fish fillets in dish, turning to coat both sides with oil. Cover with waxed paper; microwave on 100% (high) 4 minutes, turning fish after 2 minutes. Set fish aside.

Or, place shrimp in a 2-quart casserole. Cover with a lid or vented plastic wrap. Microwave on 100% (high) 4 minutes, rearranging shrimp after 2 minutes. Shrimp is done when it turns opaque.

To make Salsa Roja, place remaining 1 tablespoon oil, tomato paste, water, onion, garlic, chile powder, oregano, cominos and salt in a blender or food processor. Process until pureed. Pour mixture into a 1-quart bowl. Cover with waxed paper; microwave on 70% (medium-high) 10 minutes, stirring every 3 minutes.

Pour cooked salsa over cooked fish. Cover with waxed paper; microwave on 70% (medium-high) 2 minutes. Fish is cooked if it flakes easily. Serve immediately with lime or lemon wedges.

Caldillo de Pescado

Fish Soup

Enjoy your favorite seafood in this delicious soup.

Power level: high
Cooking time: 33 minutes
Servings: 6

2 tablespoons olive oil
1/4 cup chopped onion
2 garlic cloves, chopped
2 medium tomatoes, chopped
1/2 cup finely chopped celery
1 teaspoon azafrán
1 teaspoon dried leaf oregano
1/2 teaspoon cilantro seeds, crushed

1 tablespoon red chile powder
1/2 teaspoon salt
2 (8-oz.) bottles clam juice
3 cups water
2 lbs. fish and shellfish
1/4 cup fresh cilantro or parsley leaves
1 lime, quartered

Use any combination of white fish, rock fish, shelled and veined shrimp, crab legs broken into 3-inch segments, scallops, clams or mussels. Combine oil, onions and garlic in a 5-quart casserole. Cover with a lid; microwave on 100% (high) 3 minutes. Add tomatoes, celery, azafrán, oregano, cilantro seeds, chile powder, salt, clam juice and water. Cover with a lid; microwave on 100% (high) 15 minutes. Add fish and shellfish. Cover and microwave on 100% (high) 15 minutes or until clams and/or mussels open.

To serve, fill individual bowls with Caldillo. Garnish with fresh cilantro or parsley and a squeeze of lime.

When traveling in Mexico, my husband would always make a special trip to a seafood restaurant in Guaymas, Sonora to have this soup. It is similar to bouillabaisse. After his raving about this soup, I felt I should honor his appetite by recreating it at home.

Camarones con Verduras

Shrimp with Vegetables

Power level: high
Cooking time: 10 minutes
Servings: 4 to 5

2 tablespoons olive oil	1 teaspoon paprika
1/2 cup chopped onion	1/4 teaspoon dried leaf oregano
2 garlic cloves, chopped	1/2 teaspoon salt
1 medium tomato, chopped	1 tablespoon lime or lemon juice
1/2 cup chopped bell pepper	1 lb. medium shrimp, peeled and veined
1/4 cup chopped green chiles	1 lime, quartered

Place all ingredients except shrimp and lime into a 2-quart casserole. Cover with waxed paper; microwave on 100% (high) 4 minutes, stirring after 2 minutes. Stir in shrimp. Cover with waxed paper; microwave on 100% (high) 5 minutes, stirring after 2-1/2 minutes. Shrimp is done when it turns opaque. Squeeze lime over shrimp dish. Serve immediately.

COMIDAS de VERDURAS

Vegetable dishes in traditional Mexican cuisine were usually served with a cheese sauce. Vegetables were also added to meat dishes or were simmered and used as a topping for meats, poultry or fish dishes.

White cheese, a Mexican tradition, was commonly made from "leche cuajada" or curdled milk. A pouch was made of "manta" or muslin or several layers of cheese cloth. The curdled milk was poured into the pouch and hung in the coolest part of the house. Whey was permitted to drip into a bucket for 3 to 4 days until a white mass of cheese formed in the pouch. At that time, a sweet, white, pear-shape cheese was removed. This sweet cheese was used to make quesadillas, served with fruits or added to vegetables.

Even today, you can buy white cheese and goat cheese in the old markets of Juárez, Mexico. They have been long-standing favorites in Mexican cooking.

At our house, we almost always had cheese in our vegetable dishes, whether it was squash, corn or green beans. I particularly liked thinly sliced summer squash with cheese. Today, I generally use Monterey Jack or mild Cheddar cheese in my recipes.

Baking was a common method of preparing vegetables and fruits. Included were such favorites as Manzanas Asadas or Baked Apples, and Baked Plátanos or plantains. The plantain is a cousin to the banana. Plantains are larger and more firm than bananas and not as sweet, but more starchy. Plantains are rich in vitamin C and potassium.

Berenjena y Chile con Queso

Eggplant & Chile Cheese

The combination of eggplant, cheese and chiles makes this vegetable dish a hit at mealtime.

Power level: high, medium-high
Cooking time: 21 to 23 minutes
Servings: 6

1 large eggplant
1/2 cup water
1 egg
1/4 cup chopped onion
2 cups fresh bread crumbs
1/2 teaspoon salt
1/4 teaspoon pepper

1/4 teaspoon dried leaf oregano, crushed
1/4 teaspoon paprika
1 cup shredded Cheddar cheese (4 oz.)
1/2 cup chopped green chiles or
    1 (4-oz.) can diced green chiles
4 bacon slices, cut in quarters

Peel eggplant; cut in cubes. You should have about 4 cups. Place eggplant cubes and water in a 1-1/2-quart casserole. Cover with waxed paper; microwave on 100% (high) 9 minutes. Let stand 5 minutes. Drain off liquid; mash eggplant. In a large bowl, combine mashed eggplant, egg, onion, bread crumbs, salt, pepper, oregano, paprika, cheese and chiles; blend well. Set mixture aside.

Butter a microwave-safe ring mold or a round, 1-1/2-quart casserole. Place an inverted custard cup in center of casserole. Pour eggplant mixture into buttered ring mold or casserole. Top mixture with bacon strips. Cover with waxed paper; microwave on 70% (medium-high) 12 minutes, rotating dish after 6 minutes. Let stand 5 minutes. Casserole is done when a wooden pick inserted in center comes out clean. If more cooking is needed, cover with waxed paper; microwave on 70% (medium-high) 2 minutes or until done. Serve immediately.

Cacerola de Habas y Chile

Lima Bean & Chile Casserole

Chile powder blends with vegetables for a great taste.

Power level: high
Cooking time: 14 to 16 minutes
Servings: 6

8 bacon slices
1 tablespoon bacon drippings or
    vegetable shortening
1/4 cup chopped onion
1/4 cup chopped bell pepper
1 garlic clove, chopped

1 (10-oz.) pkg. frozen lima beans
2 cups Stewed Tomatoes, page 4, or
    1 (16-oz.) can stewed tomatoes
1 tablespoon red chile powder
1/4 teaspoon salt
1/4 teaspoon ground oregano

Place bacon in a microwave browning dish or casserole. Cover with paper towel; microwave on 100% (high) 4 minutes, turning bacon after 2 minutes. If bacon is not cooked, turn bacon again. Cover and microwave on 100% (high) another 2 minutes or until bacon is crisp. Remove bacon, reserving drippings. Pat bacon between paper towels to remove excess fat; dice bacon.

Combine 1 tablespoon reserved bacon drippings or shortening, onion, bell pepper and garlic in a 1-1/2-quart casserole. Cover with waxed paper; microwave on 100% (high) 2 minutes. Stir in lima beans, tomatoes, chile powder, salt, oregano and cooked bacon. Cover with waxed paper; microwave on 100% (high) 8 minutes, stirring after 4 minutes. Let stand 5 minutes. Casserole is done when lima beans are tender. If more cooking is needed, cover with waxed paper; microwave on 100% (high) 3 to 4 minutes or until done. Serve hot.

Calabaza con Queso

Squash with Cheese

If you grow squash in your garden, here's a wonderful dish that is easy to prepare and tastes great!

Power level: high
Cooking time: 15 minutes
Servings: 6

2 tablespoons butter or margarine
1/4 cup chopped onion
1 garlic clove, chopped
1/4 cup chopped bell pepper
3 cups thinly sliced summer squash,
   such as zucchini, cocozelle or straight
   or crooked-neck squash

1/2 teaspoon salt
1/2 cup water
1 cup shredded Monterey Jack or
   jalapeño cheese (4 oz.)

Combine butter or margarine, onion, garlic and bell pepper in a 2-quart casserole. Cover with waxed paper; microwave on 100% (high) 3 minutes. Stir in squash, salt and water. Cover with waxed paper; microwave on 100% (high) 10 minutes, stirring after 5 minutes. Squash should be tender. If more cooking is needed, cover with waxed paper; microwave on 100% (high) 2 minutes or until tender.

Drain liquid from squash; stir in 1/2 cup cheese. Sprinkle remaining cheese over squash. Cover with waxed paper; microwave on 100% (high) 2 minutes. Serve hot.

❦   ❦   ❦

In the early 1920s, the Amador Hotel in Las Cruces, New Mexico, was the showplace of the South-
west with its plush European decor and little theater. Many famous people from the Eastern United
States stayed there on their way to Mexico or the West Coast. The magician Houdini, General John
Pershing, John Dean of the New York opera fame and a number of Hollywood celebrities were among
the guests.

The Amador Hotel had a varied cuisine, from Mexican to Continental. My great-aunt Lupe, who
was their cook for several years, often told me that their most requested dish was her Calabaza con
Queso. Calabaza, squash or pumpkin in any form, was very popular.

Lupe told of an hilarious occasion when the owner of the Amador Hotel brought her two packets of
dehydrated carrots, thinking them to be pumpkin. She asked Lupe to make the guests a pumpkin pie.
Lupe soaked the dehydrated carrots, sliced and spiced them until she got them to taste as close to
pumpkin as possible. Well, the guests were so thrilled with the pie that several of them begged her to
share her secret recipe with them!

Chile con Elote

Chile with Corn

Creamed corn gives this dish a creamy consistency when baked. It's a fine dish to accompany any Mexican entree.

Power level: high, medium-high
Cooking time: 17 to 18 minutes
Servings: 6

2 tablespoons butter or margarine
1/4 cup chopped onion
1/4 cup chopped bell pepper
2 tablespoons all-purpose flour
1/2 teaspoon salt
1/2 teaspoon paprika

1/2 cup chopped green chiles
1 egg
1 (8-oz.) can cream-style corn
1 (16-oz.) can whole-kernel corn, drained
1/2 cup shredded Cheddar cheese (2 oz.)

Combine butter or margarine, onion and bell pepper in a 1-1/2-quart casserole. Cover with waxed paper; microwave on 100% (high) 2 minutes. Stir in flour, salt, paprika, chiles, egg and corn. Cover with waxed paper; microwave on 70% (medium-high) 14 to 15 minutes, stirring after 7 minutes. Top with cheese; microwave on 70% (medium-high) 1 minute. Let stand 5 minutes before serving.

Cacerola de Elote

Corn Casserole

Enjoy a hearty meal in itself. Serve with fresh beans and warm flour tortillas.

Power level: high, medium-high
Cooking time: 16 to 17 minutes
Servings: 4

1 lb. ground beef
2 tablespoons butter or margarine
1 (8-3/4-oz.) can whole-kernel corn, drained
1/4 cup yellow cornmeal
1/2 teaspoon salt
1/4 teaspoon ground oregano

1/2 teaspoon onion powder
1/4 cup dairy sour cream
1/2 cup all-purpose flour
1/2 teaspoon baking powder
1/4 cup chopped green chiles
1/2 cup shredded Cheddar cheese (2 oz.)

Crumble ground beef into a 1-1/2-quart casserole or microwave browning dish. Cover with waxed paper; microwave on 100% (high) 4 to 5 minutes, stirring after 2 minutes. Meat is done when it is no longer pink in color. Drain off fat; set aside.

Place butter or margarine in a glass bowl; microwave on 100% (high) 45 seconds or until melted. Stir in corn, cornmeal, salt, oregano, onion powder and sour cream. Process mixture in a blender or food processor until smooth.

Pour blended ingredients into a large bowl; stir in flour and baking powder. Add cooked ground beef and chiles; stir well.

Grease a microwave-safe ring mold or round, glass cake dish. Place an inverted custard cup in center of cake dish. Pour batter into greased ring mold or cake dish. Cover with waxed paper; microwave on 70% (medium-high) 10 minutes, turning dish after 5 minutes. Sprinkle cheese over corn mixture. Cover with waxed paper; microwave on 70% (medium-high) 1 minute. Let stand 5 minutes. Serve hot.

Ensalada Mexicana

Taco Salad

If you enjoy salads, try this protein-rich "meal-in-a-salad."

Power level: high, medium-high
Cooking time: 10 minutes
Servings: 6

1 lb. lean ground beef
3 tablespoons Taco Seasoning Mix, page
    7, or use 1 (1-1/4-oz.) pkg. taco
    seasoning mix
1-1/2 cups cooked Pinto Beans, drained,
    page 68, or 1 (15-oz.) can pinto beans
1 small head lettuce
2 tomatoes, chopped
1/2 cup chopped bell pepper

1/3 cup chopped onion
1/3 cup chopped celery
1/2 cup sliced ripe olives
1 cup shredded Cheddar cheese (4 oz.)
6 cups Tortilla Chips, page 50, or
    1 (11-oz.) bag tortilla chips, plain
    or flavored
1 cup Taco Sauce, page 7

Crumble ground beef into a 2-quart casserole. Cover with waxed paper; microwave on 100% (high) 5 minutes, stirring after 2-1/2 minutes. Drain off fat; stir in seasoning mix and pinto beans. Cover with waxed paper; microwave meat mixture on 70% (medium-high) 5 minutes.

Wash lettuce; pat between paper towels to absorb excess moisture. When dry, tear lettuce into pieces; place in a large bowl. Add tomatoes, bell pepper, onion, celery, 1/4 cup olives and 1/2 cup cheese; toss together. Push salad to edge of bowl, leaving a well in the middle. Spoon meat mixture into center of salad. Top with remaining olives and cheese.

Place tortilla chips around edge of meat mixture. Serve remaining chips in a separate bowl with Taco Sauce.

Plátanos Dulces

Candied Plantains

If you are unable to find the Mexican-type banana referred to as a plantain, firm nearly ripe bananas can be used.

Power level: high
Cooking time: 8 minutes
Servings: 4

2 plantains
3 tablespoons butter or margarine
3 tablespoons brown sugar
3 tablespoons granulated sugar

Peel plantains; cut lengthwise into quarters. Cut each quarter into 3-inch pieces; set aside. Place butter or margarine in a glass pie plate. Cover with waxed paper; microwave on 100% (high) 1 minute or until melted. Add plantain pieces. Cover with waxed paper; microwave on 100% (high) 6 minutes, turning pieces over after 3 minutes. Sprinkle with brown sugar and granulated sugar. Microwave, uncovered, on 100% (high) 1 minute. Let stand 5 minutes. Plantain pieces should be soft when pierced with a fork. If more cooking is needed, cover and microwave on 100% (high) 1 minute or until tender. Serve warm.

Tip

If plantains are green, let stand at room temperature until brown and starting to soften. Ripening may take several days.

Plátanos al Horno

Baked Plantains

A sweet-cream mixture is spooned over baked plantains for a creamy sweet flavor.

Power level: high, medium-high
Cooking time: 8 minutes
Servings: 4

2 plantains	**1/4 teaspoon ground cinnamon**
3 tablespoons butter or margarine	**1/4 teaspoon ground nutmeg**
1/3 cup lightly packed brown sugar	**2 tablespoons half and half**

Peel plantains; cut lengthwise into quarters. Cut each quarter into 3-inch pieces; set pieces aside.

Put butter or margarine in a glass pie plate. Cover with waxed paper; microwave on 100% (high) 1 minute or until melted. Stir in brown sugar, cinnamon, nutmeg and half and half.

Place plantain pieces in glass pie plate; spoon sugar mixture over plantains. Cover with waxed paper; microwave on 70% (medium-high) 7 to 8 minutes, rearranging pieces after 3-1/2 minutes. Let stand 5 minutes. Plantain pieces should be soft when pierced with a fork. If more cooking is needed, cover and microwave on 70% (medium-high) 1 minute or until pieces are tender. Serve warm.

Variation

After plantain pieces have been baked, add 2 tablespoons rum; allow rum to soak into plantain 1 minute. Then serve.

Ejotes con Queso

Green Beans with Cheese

This is a colorful and delicious vegetable dish.

Power level: high
Cooking time: 5 to 6 minutes
Servings: 4

2 tablespoons vegetable oil
1/4 cup chopped onion
1 garlic clove, chopped
1/4 teaspoon dried leaf oregano, crushed
1 (16-oz.) can whole green beans, drained

1/4 teaspoon salt
1/4 cup chopped green chiles
1 cup shredded Monterey Jack cheese
  (4 oz.)
1 tomato, cut into wedges

Combine oil, onion, garlic and oregano in a 1-1/2-quart casserole. Cover with waxed paper; microwave on 100% (high) 2 minutes. Stir in green beans, salt, chiles and 1/2 cup cheese. Cover with waxed paper; microwave on 100% (high) 3 minutes.

Arrange tomato wedges on top of green beans; sprinkle with remaining cheese. Cover with waxed paper; microwave on 100% (high) 45 seconds or until cheese melts. Serve hot.

Barquitos de Oro

Little Golden Boats

Prepared in this manner, these yams give the appearance of little yellow boats.

Power level: high
Cooking time: 7 to 8 minutes
Servings: 2

1 yam (about 3/4 lb.)	**2 tablespoons roasted piñones or**
1/4 teaspoon ground cinnamon	**chopped blanched almonds**
1/4 cup whipping cream	**1/2 cup whipped cream**
1 tablespoon drained crushed pineapple	

Scrub yam; pierce with a fork to prevent rupture during baking. Place in a glass pie plate; microwave on 100% (high) 7 to 8 minutes, turning yam over after 3-1/2 minutes. Yam is cooked when it can be pierced easily with a fork. If more cooking is needed, microwave on 100% (high) 1 minute or until tender. Let yam cool.

Cut cooled, cooked yam in half, lengthwise. Scoop out flesh, placing it in a small bowl; reserve hollowed out skins. Stir cinnamon and whipping cream into flesh. Whip until mixture is very light. Stir in pineapple and nuts. Spoon mixture back into yam-skin shells. Chill boats 15 minutes or until ready to serve. To serve, top with whipped cream.

In my recipe Little Golden Bowls, I use piñon nuts. There is a tradition of using piñon nuts harvested from the pine forests of the Southwest. My mother recalls her grandmother getting piñon nuts from an old man named Don Atenójenes. She would give the man a 50- to 100-pound sack of dried corn to take with him to the mountains of Northern New Mexico. The corn was to put out for the squirrels as food to compensate for our harvest of piñones. He would faithfully return with a 100-pound sack of piñones which would last for a year.

My mother's job was to separate chaff from nuts, which she would do on a very windy day. She would take a pail of piñones and pour them from a height of 3 to 4 feet, letting them fall into a large tub. The wind would in turn blow away any dried leaves, sticks, sand or other foreign material. Grandmother would then spread the piñones on a table where any other foreign particles would be removed by hand.

Piñones were then roasted in big, square roasting pans in the kitchen wood-stove oven under the watchful eye of her grandmother. Grandmother would stir the nuts with a long-handled spoon to keep them from burning. The aroma of roasting piñones was a lasting pleasant memory of my mother's.

After the roasting, her grandmother would sell the nuts in quarter-pound sacks for a nickel, half-pound sacks for a dime, and pound sacks for a quarter. A paper sack of freshly roasted piñones was a must for neighborhood football fans for a hometown game.

While teaching in San Rafael in Northern New Mexico, I thought I could engage my family in collecting piñones. My students told me of a piñon grove and their practice of putting out grain for the squirrels when gathering piñones. With a sheet, bucket and a bag of grain, we set out to harvest nuts. We learned that the piñon trees do not always bear a bumper crop. We returned empty-handed, but the squirrels ate well that autumn.

Camotes Dulces

Candied Yams

Cooking yams at a low setting allows the sugar mixture to crystallize.

Power level: high, medium-low, medium-high
Cooking time: 37 minutes
Servings: 6

1-1/2 lbs. yams
1/2 cup water
1/3 cup lightly packed brown sugar
1/3 cup granulated sugar

Scrub yams; cut into 1/2-inch-thick cross-sectional slices. Place yam slices and water in a 2-1/2-quart casserole. Cover with waxed paper; microwave on 100% (high) 12 minutes, rearranging slices after 6 minutes. Yam slices should be tender when pierced with a fork. Cool slices about 15 minutes. Peel skins from slices; set slices aside.

Butter a 12" x 8" flat-bottom casserole. Combine brown sugar and granulated sugar in a small bowl. Dip each slice into sugar mixture; arrange slices in rows in buttered casserole. Microwave, uncovered, on 30% (medium-low) 15 minutes. Rotate dish; microwave on 70% (medium-high) 10 minutes. Let stand 5 minutes. Serve hot or cold.

Tip

Sweet potatoes and yams are generally considered interchangeable terms, yet there really is a difference in these two vegetables. True yams are generally sweeter and wetter than sweet potatoes. Sweet potatoes are either moist-fleshed or dry-fleshed. Dry-fleshed sweet potatoes have a light-yellow flesh and resemble a regular baking potato after cooking. Moist-fleshed sweet potatoes, often referred to as yams, range from a reddish-orange to dark red and purple.

PANES, POSTRES y BEBIDAS

A shopping trip to Juárez was one of my childhood delights. I particularly liked going to the candy vendors in the mercado. I remember standing on my tiptoes and surveying all the different colorful candies. There would be "dulce de coco" or coconut candy, various types of "jamoncillos" or fudge candies and "penuche," a brown-sugar fudge among others. My search would usually continue until I spotted my favorite, an anise-flavored candy stick called "melcocha." One stick of melcocha would last the whole trip home.

No neighborhood was complete without a "panadería" or bakery. The aroma of the little loaves and sweet breads would attract the attention of the neighborhood. I remember the piles of "pan dulce" in the bakery display case. Pan dulce came in an array of shapes and colors. There would be "cuernitos" or crescent-shaped sweet rolls, "empanadas" or turnovers, "polvorones" or shortbread cookies, "rosquitas" or doughnut-shaped cookies and "pan de huevo" or egg-topped sweet rolls. Each had its own colored sweetened egg topping: pinks, yellows and whites.

Although baking bread in a microwave takes time and patience, Pan de Huevo, pages 130–131, is worth the time and effort.

Pan de Huevo

Egg-Topped Sweet Rolls

Breads will not brown in the microwave, but the rich color of egg topping gives these sweet rolls an attractive appearance. Serve these delicious rolls with coffee.

Power level: high, low, medium-high
Cooking time: 35 minutes
Servings: 12

Dough

1 cup warm milk
2 (1/4-oz.) pkgs. active dry yeast
   (about 2 tablespoons)
3/4 cup sugar

2 tablespoons vegetable oil
2 eggs
1 teaspoon salt
4-1/2 cups all-purpose flour

Topping

2 eggs, separated
1-1/2 cups all-purpose flour
3/4 cup sugar
1-1/2 teaspoons ground cinnamon

1/4 teaspoon salt
1/2 cup butter or margarine
2 tablespoons water

For dough, microwave milk in a large glass bowl on 100% (high) 1 minute or until lukewarm. Stir in yeast; let stand 5 minutes or until foamy.

Combine sugar, oil, eggs and salt in a separate bowl; add to milk mixture along with 2 cups flour. Beat mixture with an electric mixer at medium speed 3 minutes. Stir in enough remaining flour to form a stiff dough. Knead dough on a lightly floured board 7 minutes. Clean and grease bowl; return dough to bowl, turning to grease all sides. Set dough aside.

Pour about 3 cups water in a shallow dish that is large enough to hold the large bowl of dough. Microwave water on 100% (high) 4 minutes. Set bowl of dough into dish of hot water. Brush dough lightly with vegetable oil. Cover with waxed paper; microwave on 10% (low) 10 minutes. Let dough stand in microwave 15 minutes or until doubled in bulk.

Grease 2 (13" x 9") casseroles. Remove dough from bowl; divide into 12 equal balls. Place 6 dough balls in each dish, making 2 rows of 3 dough balls each. Form rolls by pressing each dough ball flat until edges of dough are touching each other.

For topping, combine egg yolks, flour, sugar, cinnamon and salt in a small bowl. Cut butter or margarine into mixture using a pastry blender or fork. Set egg mixture aside.

In a small bowl, blend together egg whites and 2 tablespoons water. Brush egg-white mixture on top of each roll. Spread egg topping over top of egg-white mixture on each roll. Use all the egg topping. Cut a criss-cross design in top of each roll with a knife. Cover rolls with waxed paper.

Reheat shallow dish with water on 100% (high) 5 minutes or until water boils. Place one of the casseroles containing 6 rolls on top of the shallow dish of hot water. Microwave rolls on 10% (low) 10 minutes or until rolls double in bulk. Repeat procedure for other dish of rolls. Remove dish of hot water from microwave.

To bake rolls, place one dish of rolls on an inverted dish in microwave. Cover with waxed paper; microwave on 70% (medium-high) 8 to 10 minutes, rotating dish every 4 minutes. Let rolls stand 5 minutes. A wooden pick inserted in rolls should come out clean. If more baking is needed, cover with waxed paper; microwave on 70% (medium-high) 2 minutes or until rolls are done. Remove rolls from casserole; cool on a rack. Repeat for remaining dish of rolls.

Flan

Caramel Custard

Flan is served as a molded custard, topped with a caramel sauce. Be careful not to overcook the sugar mixture because the caramel will crystallize before it can coat the custard cups.

Power level: high, medium
Cooking time: 24 minutes
Servings: 4

1/2 cup sugar	1/3 cup sugar
1/3 cup water	1 teaspoon vanilla extract
2 cups milk	2 teaspoons cornstarch
3 eggs	1/8 teaspoon salt

To make caramel coating for custard cups, combine 1/2 cup sugar and 1/3 cup water in a glass bowl. Microwave on 100% (high) 6 to 7 minutes, stirring after 3 minutes. Caramel mixture is ready when it is golden in color. Pour equal amounts of caramel mixture into each of 4 custard cups. Rotate each cup so caramel coats side and bottom of each cup; set cups aside. Heat milk in a separate glass bowl on 100% (high) 3 minutes. Beat together eggs, 1/3 cup sugar, vanilla, cornstarch and salt in a small glass bowl. Slowly blend egg mixture into heated milk. Set milk-egg mixture aside.

Pour about 1-1/2 cups water into an 8-inch-square flat-bottom casserole; microwave on 100% (high) 4 minutes or until water begins to boil. Leave casserole with hot water in microwave. Pour milk-egg mixture into caramel-coated custard cups. Set each custard cup in hot water in microwave. Cover entire casserole with waxed paper; microwave on 50% (medium) 15 to 16 minutes, rotating casserole every 5 minutes. Let custard cups stand 5 minutes in hot water. Insert a knife into flan; if it comes out clean, flan is done. Refrigerate until cool.

To unmold cooled flan, invert each custard cup onto a dessert plate so that caramel coating is on top of flan. Lift custard cup from flan. If flan does not dislodge when cup is lifted, run a sharp knife between flan and side of custard cup; then invert. Refrigerate flan until ready to serve.

Creamy Flan

Caramel Custard

Sweetened condensed milk makes this flan smooth and creamy, and very easy to prepare.

Power level: high, medium
Cooking time: 20 to 22 minutes
Servings: 4

1/2 cup sugar
1/3 cup water
1 cup Sweetened Condensed Milk, page
    138, or commercial sweetened
    condensed milk

1 cup half and half
2 teaspoons cornstarch
3 eggs
1 teaspoon vanilla extract
1/8 teaspoon salt

Prepare caramel and coat custard cups as in Flan, page 132. Combine sweetened condensed milk, half and half and cornstarch in a glass bowl. Microwave on 100% (high) 4 minutes or until mixture is hot but not boiling. Set hot milk aside.

Break eggs into a small bowl; add vanilla and salt. Beat well. Gradually add egg mixture to hot milk, stirring constantly; set mixture aside.

Heat water and bake custard as in Flan, page 132, reducing cooking time on 50% (medium) to 10 to 11 minutes, rotating casserole every 4 minutes. Finish as directed.

Flan is a recipe that dates back to the period of the Spanish Conquistadores. Its popularity continues to grow. You can use other flavorings or add grated coconut to the mixture before cooking. As an added garnish, top each serving with a tablespoon of meringue or whipped cream. Sprinkle with crushed pecans.

Arroz con Leche

Rice Pudding

Serve this creamy rice pudding hot or cold.

Power level: high
Cooking time: 14 minutes
Servings: 4

1 cup uncooked quick-cooking rice	**1/2 cup milk**
1 cup water	**1/2 cup sugar**
1/4 teaspoon salt	**1/2 teaspoon vanilla extract**
1 tablespoon butter or margarine	**1/2 cup raisins, if desired**
1 egg	**Ground cinnamon**

Combine rice, water, salt and butter or margarine in a 1-1/2-quart casserole. Cover with a lid; microwave on 100% (high) 8 minutes or until water is absorbed and rice is tender. Let stand 5 minutes.

Beat together egg, milk, sugar and vanilla in a small bowl. Add egg mixture and raisins, if desired, to cooked rice; stir well to blend. Cover with waxed paper; microwave on 100% (high) 6 minutes, stirring every 2 minutes. Pour rice pudding into 4 dessert dishes; sprinkle with cinnamon. Serve warm or chilled.

Capirotada

Bread Pudding

Bread pudding is a family favorite, especially during the holiday season.

Power level: high
Cooking time: 11 minutes
Servings: 6

3/4 cup lightly packed brown sugar
1-1/2 cups water
1/2 cup raisins
1 egg
1/2 teaspoon vanilla extract
2 tablespoons powdered sugar

5 slices of white bread, cut into cubes
1/2 cup pecans pieces
1 cup shredded mild Cheddar cheese
  (4 oz.)
2 tablespoons butter or margarine

Combine brown sugar and water in a glass bowl; microwave on 100% (high) 5 minutes Add raisins to hot mixture; soak raisins 5 minutes.

Beat together egg, vanilla and powdered sugar in a small bowl. Add egg mixture to raisin mixture, stirring to blend; set mixture aside.

In a 1-1/2-quart casserole, alternately layer bread cubes, raisin mixture, pecans and cheese. Repeat layers. Before final layer of cheese is added, dot with butter or margarine; then add remaining cheese. Cover with waxed paper; microwave on 100% (high) 6 minutes, rotating dish after 3 minutes. Let stand 5 minutes. Serve hot or cold.

Capirotada was a standard for the holidays. My mother would prepare Capirotada in a large pan, making enough for family and friends who would stop by to wish us Feliz Navidad, a Merry Christmas. As much as I enjoyed the company, I would hide some Capirotada in the refrigerator for enjoying the next day. My recipe is an adaptation of my mother's recipe.

Natillas

A smooth custard pudding, especially nice served with a slice of fresh juicy pineapple.

Power level: high
Cooking time: 7 minutes
Servings: 6

2 cups milk
1/2 cup sugar
3 eggs, separated
2 tablespoons cornstarch
Pinch of salt

1-1/2 teaspoons vanilla extract
1/4 teaspoon cream of tartar
1 tablespoon sugar
Ground cinnamon or ground nutmeg

Combine milk, 1/2 cup sugar, egg yolks, cornstarch and salt in a 2-quart casserole; beat with a whisk until blended. Cover with waxed paper; microwave on 100% (high) 7 minutes or until thickened, stirring every 2 minutes. Stir in vanilla; set aside.

Beat egg whites in a small bowl, gradually adding cream of tartar and 1 tablespoon sugar, until egg whites are stiff. Fold beaten egg whites into pudding mixture. Pour pudding mixture into 6 individual serving dishes. Refrigerate until cooled and set. To serve, sprinkle with cinnamon or nutmeg.

Natillas de Chocolate

Mexican Chocolate Pudding

Makes a delicious dessert in no time.

Power level: high
Cooking time: 8 minutes
Servings: 6

2 (1-oz.) squares semisweet chocolate
2 cups milk
1/2 cup sugar
2 tablespoons cornstarch
Pinch of salt
3 eggs, separated

1/4 teaspoon ground cinnamon
1 teaspoon vanilla extract
1/4 teaspoon cream of tartar
2 tablespoons sugar
Chocolate shavings, if desired

Combine chocolate and 1 cup milk in a 2 quart casserole. Microwave on 100% (high) 3 minutes or until chocolate melts. Add remaining milk, 1/2 cup sugar, cornstarch, salt, egg yolks and cinnamon; beat with a whisk until smooth. Cover with waxed paper; microwave on 100% (high) 5 minutes or until thickened, stirring after 2-1/2 minutes. Stir in vanilla; set aside.

Beat egg whites in a small bowl, gradually adding cream of tartar and 2 tablespoons sugar, until egg whites are stiff. Fold beaten egg whites into pudding mixture. Pour pudding mixture into 6 individual dishes. Refrigerate until cooled and set. Serve topped with chocolate shavings, if desired.

Leche Dulce Condensada

Sweetened Condensed Milk

This recipe is easy and economical to prepare. Use it for any of your recipes calling for sweetened condensed milk.

Power level: high
Cooking time: 3 minutes
Servings: 1-2/3 cups

1 cup sugar
1/2 cup water
1/3 cup butter or margarine
1-1/2 cups dry milk powder

Combine sugar, water and butter or margarine in a glass bow1. Microwave on 100% (high) 3 minutes, stirring after 1-1/2 minutes. Pour hot mixture into a blender. Add powdered milk; process thoroughly. Refrigerate condensed milk. Mixture will thicken as it cools. Use in any recipe calling for sweetened condensed milk.

Cajeta

Caramel Candy

Literally translated, Cajeta means "in a box."

Power level: high
Cooking time: 26 minutes
Servings: 1-1/4 cups

1-3/4 cups milk
1 cup granulated sugar
1/2 cup light corn syrup

1 teaspoon cornstarch
1/4 teaspoon baking soda

Pour milk into a 5-quart glass bowl. Microwave uncovered on 100% (high) 6 minutes or until milk boils. Stir in sugar, corn syrup, cornstarch and baking soda. Microwave on 100% (high) 20 minutes or until mixture thickens and becomes a golden brown, stirring every 5 minutes. Immediately remove from microwave; beat candy vigorously with a wooden spoon 2 minutes. Refrigerate until cool. Candy will thicken as it cools.

It was a common practice for people in Southern New Mexico and West Texas to shop in the mercado or market in Juárez, Mexico. If my parents were making a trip, we would beg them to bring us our special treat. That was a small, round wooden box containing our favorite soft caramel candy, "Cajeta." It was fun just to eat the caramel candy right out of the wooden box. This microwave recipe for Cajeta makes a soft caramel, great to be eaten by the spoonful or used as a sweet topping for ice cream.

Chile Pipitoria de Cacahuate

Chile Peanut Brittle

I owe my microwave Chile Peanut Brittle recipe to my dad. He likes a little chile in everything, even for a different taste in confections.

Power level: high
Cooking time: 9 minutes
Servings: about 1 pound candy

1 cup shelled, unsalted peanuts
1/4 cup flaked coconut
1 teaspoon vegetable oil
2 teaspoons red chile powder

1 cup sugar
1/2 cup light corn syrup
1 teaspoon butter or margarine
1 teaspoon baking soda

Combine peanuts, coconut, oil and chile powder in a glass pie plate. Microwave on 100% (high) 2 minutes, stirring after 1 minute; set aside.

Grease a baking sheet; set aside. Combine sugar and corn syrup in a 5-quart bowl. Microwave on 100% (high) 6 minutes, stirring after 3 minutes. Stir in butter or margarine. Microwave on 100% (high) 1 minute. Immediately stir in baking soda. Add peanut mixture; stir until light and foamy. Pour mixture onto greased baking sheet. Butter your hands or a rolling pin; flatten the candy. Let peanut brittle stand until cool; then break into pieces.

Variation

Use chopped, unsalted cashews in place of peanuts.

Dulce de Coco

Coconut Candy

If you like coconut, you'll enjoy this light, creamy coconut candy.

Power level: high
Cooking time: 17 to 18 minutes
Servings: 32 to 36 pieces

1 tablespoon vegetable oil
3 cups flaked coconut or 1 (7-oz.) pkg.
   flaked coconut
2 tablespoons butter or margarine
1 cup granulated sugar
1/4 cup light corn syrup

3/4 cup milk
1/8 teaspoon baking soda
1/8 teaspoon salt
1 teaspoon vanilla extract
1 cup unsifted powdered sugar

Pour oil into a 9-inch glass pie plate; blend in coconut. Cover with waxed paper; microwave on 100% (high) 4 minutes, stirring at 1 minute intervals. When coconut has browned, set dish aside.

Grease a baking sheet; set aside. Combine butter or margarine, granulated sugar, corn syrup, milk, baking soda and salt in a 5-quart glass bowl. Microwave on 100% (high) 13 to 14 minutes or until candy reaches soft-ball stage, stirring every 4 minutes. To test for soft-ball stage, drop about 1/4 teaspoon hot mixture into very cold water. It should form a soft ball. If using a microwave-safe candy thermometer, mixture is ready when temperature reaches 235F (115C).

When candy reaches soft-ball stage, vigorously beat in coconut, vanilla and powdered sugar with a wooden spoon. Drop by teaspoonfuls onto greased baking sheet. Cool candy before serving.

Jamoncillo de Chocolate

Chocolate Milk Fudge

If you like chocolate, you will enjoy this candy.

Power level: high
Cooking time: 6 to 7 minutes
Servings: 32 pieces

1-1/2 cups Sweetened Condensed Milk, page 138, or commercial sweetened condensed milk
1/4 cup unsweetened cocoa powder

1-1/2 cups unsifted powdered sugar
1 teaspoon vanilla extract
32 pecan halves

Grease a baking sheet; set aside. Stir together condensed milk and cocoa powder in a 5-quart casserole. Microwave, uncovered, on 100% (high) 6 to 7 minutes or until candy reaches soft-ball stage, stirring every 3 minutes. To test for soft-ball stage, drop about 1/4 teaspoon hot mixture into very cold water. It should form a soft ball. If using a microwave-safe candy thermometer, mixture is ready when temperature reaches 235F (115C).

When mixture reaches soft-ball stage, add powdered sugar and vanilla; beat vigorously with a wooden spoon until candy begins to thicken. Butter your hands. While candy is still hot, shape into 32 balls, placing each on greased baking sheet. Press a pecan half into each fudge ball. Cool well before serving.

Jamoncillo de Nuez

Vanilla Fudge with Nuts

Milk and butter give this candy a light, creamy texture.

Power level: high
Cooking time: 11 minutes
Servings: 24 pieces

1/2 cup milk
1/4 cup butter or margarine
1-1/2 cups granulated sugar
1/2 teaspoon salt

1/8 teaspoon baking soda
1 teaspoon vanilla extract
1-3/4 cups unsifted powdered sugar
24 pecan halves

Grease a baking sheet; set aside. Combine milk, butter or margarine and granulated sugar in a 5 quart glass bowl. Microwave on 100% (high), uncovered, 4 minutes. Stir in salt and baking soda; microwave on 100% (high), uncovered, 7 minutes or until candy reaches soft-ball stage, stirring after 4 minutes. To test for soft-ball stage, drop about 1/4 teaspoon hot mixture into very cold water. It should form a soft ball. If using a microwave-safe candy thermometer, mixture is ready when temperature reaches 235F (115C).

When mixture reaches soft-ball stage, stir in vanilla and powdered sugar; beat vigorously with a wooden spoon until candy begins to thicken. Butter your hands. While candy is still hot, shape into 24 balls; place on greased baking sheet. Press a pecan half into each fudge ball. Cool well before serving.

Melcocha

Mexican Anise Candy Stick

Melcocha is a traditional Mexican candy with the flavor of anise.

Power level: high
Cooking time: 9 to 10 minutes
Servings: 12 pieces

1 cup (1/2 lb.) piloncillo or 1 cup lightly
    packed dark-brown sugar
1/2 cup light corn syrup

1 tablespoon butter or margarine
1-1/2 teaspoons anise flavoring
2 teaspoons baking soda

Grease a baking sheet; set aside. To soften piloncillo, place piloncillo or brown sugar in a small bowl. Cover with waxed paper; microwave on 100% (high) 1 to 2 minutes. Crumble piloncillo or brown sugar with a fork.

Combine piloncillo or brown sugar and light corn syrup in a 5-quart bowl. Microwave, uncovered, on 100% (high) 8 minutes or until candy reaches hard-crack stage, stirring every 3 minutes. To test for hard-crack stage, drop about 1/4 teaspoon hot mixture into very cold water. It should harden and crack in the cold water. If using a microwave-safe candy thermometer, mixture is ready when temperature reaches 300F (150C).

When mixture reaches hard-crack stage, immediately add anise flavoring and baking soda. Beat vigorously with a wooden spoon until mixture is light and foamy. Pour mixture into 12 mounds on greased baking sheet. Butter your hands; roll each mound into a long tube-shaped stick. To give the candy its traditional shape, take each stick and twist to form a rope-like stick. Place candy sticks on greased baking sheet; let cool. Candy is ready when it hardens.

Penuche

Brown-Sugar Fudge Candy

Piloncillo is unrefined brown sugar in the shape of a cone. The cones come in several sizes. Dark-brown sugar is a fine substitute if you cannot find piloncillo.

Power level: high
Cooking time: 11 to 13 minutes
Servings: 1-1/2 lbs. or 25 squares

2 cups (1 lb.) piloncillo or 2 cups lightly packed dark brown sugar
1/2 cup milk
1/4 cup butter or margarine

1/8 teaspoon salt
1 teaspoon vanilla extract
1-3/4 cups unsifted powdered sugar

To soften piloncillo, place piloncillo or brown sugar in a small bowl. Cover with waxed paper; microwave on 100% (high) 1 to 2 minutes. Crumble piloncillo or brown sugar with a fork.

Combine piloncillo or brown sugar, milk, butter or margarine and salt in a 5-quart glass bowl. Microwave on 100% (high) 10 to 11 minutes or until it reaches the soft-ball stage, stirring every 3 minutes. To test for soft-ball stage, drop about 1/4 teaspoon hot mixture into very cold water. It should form a soft ball. If using a microwave-safe candy thermometer, mixture is ready when temperature reaches 235F (115C).

When candy reaches soft-ball stage, stir in vanilla and powdered sugar. Beat vigorously with a wooden spoon until candy thickens. Butter your hands; knead candy lightly. Roll candy into a 2-inch diameter roll; slice into circular pieces. Or pour candy into an 8-inch-square buttered pan. Cool and cut in pieces. Serve after candy is well cooled.

Planquetas

Pralines

This caramel candy is a Mexican favorite.

Power level: high
Cooking time: 10 to 11 minutes
Servings: about 36 pralines

1/2 cup (1/4 lb.) piloncillo or dark-brown
  sugar
1-1/2 cups Sweetened Condensed Milk,
  page 138, or commercial sweetened
  condensed milk

1 teaspoon baking soda
1/8 teaspoon salt
1 teaspoon vanilla extract
1 cup pecan halves

To soften piloncillo, place piloncillo or brown sugar in a small bowl. Cover with waxed paper; microwave on 100% (high) about 1 minute. Crumble piloncillo or brown sugar with a fork.

Grease 2 baking sheets; set aside. Combine condensed milk, piloncillo or brown sugar, baking soda and salt in a 5-quart glass bowl; beat vigorously. Microwave on 100% (high) 10 to 11 minutes or until candy reaches a soft-ball stage. To test for soft-ball stage, drop about 1/4 teaspoon hot mixture into very cold water. It should form a soft ball. If using a microwave-safe thermometer, mixture is ready when temperature reaches 235F (115C).

When candy reaches soft-ball stage, beat vigorously with a wooden spoon until candy thickens. Stir in pecan halves. Drop by tablespoonfuls onto greased baking sheets. Cool pralines. Serve or store for later use.

Pastelitos de Boda

Bride's Cookies

A traditional cookie, served for special occasions, especially weddings and holidays. For best flavor, use butter, but margarine can be substituted.

Power level: medium-high
Cooking time: 6 to 7 minutes
Servings: about 42 cookies

2 cups all-purpose flour
3/4 cup powdered sugar
1-1/2 teaspoons vanilla extract
3/4 cup butter or margarine

2 to 3 tablespoons water
1 cup chopped pecans or pecan pieces
3/4 cup powdered sugar

Grease or line with waxed paper a 12" x 8" flat-bottom casserole; set aside. Combine flour, 3/4 cup powdered sugar, vanilla and butter or margarine in a bowl. Blend with an electric mixer; gradually add 2 to 3 tablespoons water, as needed, to make a soft dough. Stir in pecans.

Shape dough into 1-inch balls. Place 12 dough balls, evenly spaced apart, in casserole.

Place casserole in microwave on top of an inverted glass bowl to assure uniform baking. Microwave on 70% (medium-high) 6 to 7 minutes, turning dish after 3 minutes. Cookies are done when a wooden pick inserted in center comes out clean. Roll cookies in remaining 3/4 cup powdered sugar. Cool on a rack. Repeat baking process with remaining dough.

Bizcochitos

Anise Cookies

Combining wine or orange juice with anise gives these crispy cookies a unique flavor.

Power level: medium-high
Cooking time: 6 to 7 minutes
Servings: 30 to 32 cookies

1/2 cup lard or vegetable shortening	1/2 teaspoon baking powder
1/2 cup sugar	1/2 teaspoon salt
1 egg	3 tablespoons wine or orange juice
2 teaspoons anise seeds, crushed, or anise flavoring	1/2 cup sugar
2 cups all-purpose flour	1 teaspoon ground cinnamon

Using an electric mixer, cream together lard or shortening, 1/2 cup sugar, egg and anise seeds or flavoring in a large bowl until mixture is light and fluffy. Set mixture aside.

Combine flour, baking powder and salt in a small bowl; gradually add to creamed mixture along with wine or juice. Beat until a soft dough forms. In a small bowl, combine 1/2 cup sugar and cinnamon; set aside.

Grease or line with waxed paper a 12" x 8" flat-bottom casserole. Shape dough into 1-inch balls. Place 12 dough balls, evenly spaced apart, in casserole. Flatten each ball with the bottom of a glass until dough is about 1/4-inch thick.

Place casserole in microwave on top of an inverted glass bowl to assure uniform baking. Microwave on 70% (medium-high) 6 to 7 minutes, turning dish after 3 minutes. Cookies are done when a wooden pick inserted in center comes out clean.

Immediately after removing from oven, dip cookies in cinnamon-sugar mixture; cool on a rack. Repeat baking and coating steps for remaining cookies.

Mexican Cocoa

This is a delicious hot drink for all occasions.

Power level: high
Cooking time: 3 to 4 minutes
Servings: 4 cups

2 (1-oz.) squares semisweet chocolate
4 cups milk
2 tablespoons sugar

1/4 teaspoon ground cinnamon
1/8 teaspoon ground nutmeg
Pinch of salt

Combine all ingredients in a 4-cup glass measuring cup. Microwave on 100% (high) 3 to 4 minutes until hot and chocolate is melted. Blend with a whisk. Serve hot.

The only variety store in our neighborhood was my great-aunt Lupe's tienda, located on the street corner near our house. There were various sundries for the customers, including a large assortment of penny candy for the neighborhood kids. On her candy counter she had a large cookie jar filled with "Bizcochitos" or anise cookies. Every Saturday she would have Doña Lucia, an elderly friend, come and bake Bizcochitos for the store. I never hesitated at the chance to lend a hand. My job was to dip the freshly baked thin cookies into the cinnamon-sugar mixture. I enjoyed doing this because I could easily sneak a Bizcochito when I thought no one was looking.

Without fail, Bizcochitos and Pastelitos de Bodas were served at birthday parties, baptisms, weddings and other social occasions. Enjoy them with a cup of Mexican Cocoa.

Lupe's Champurrado

Lupe's Chocolate Corn Drink

My great-aunt Lupe was known for her Champurrado, which she often served with Pan de Huevo, pages 130–131. This is her recipe.

Power level: high, medium-high
Cooking time: 10 minutes
Servings: about 3 cups

2-1/2 cups water	**1/4 teaspoon anise flavoring**
2 (3-inch) cinnamon sticks	**1/2 cup whipping cream**
3 tablespoons masa harina	**Whipped cream, if desired**
5 tablespoons sugar	
3 tablespoons unsweetened cocoa powder	
or 1 (1-oz.) square unsweetened chocolate	

Pour water and cinnamon sticks in a 2-quart glass bowl. Cover with waxed paper; microwave on 100% (high) 5 minutes or until water begins to boil. Let stand 5 minutes. Strain cinnamon-flavored water into a 2-quart measuring cup; discard cinnamon sticks. Add masa harina, sugar and cocoa or chocolate to cinnamon water; beat with a whisk until well blended.

Cover measuring cup with waxed paper; microwave on 70% (medium-high) 5 minutes, stirring after 2-1/2 minutes. Add anise flavoring and 1/2 cup whipping cream; beat with an electric mixer at medium speed 1 minute. Pour mixture into cups or mugs for serving. Top with whipped cream, if desired. A cinnamon stick can be added for a swizzle.

Corn drinks have always been popular in Mexico. The addition of cinnamon and chocolate was common in Mexican beverages. My mother's favorite was "Champurrado." Preparation for Champurrado included wrapping a cinnamon stick and crushed anise seed in a cheese cloth, then allowing it to steep in hot water until the flavors flowed through. Although masa harina is used to thicken this beverage, it is not a thick consistency. It is a light drink.

Café Mexicano

Mexican Coffee

An excellent beverage for breakfast or after an evening meal.

Power level: high
Cooking time: 5 minutes
Servings: 2

2 cups water
2 tablespoons piloncillo or dark-brown
    sugar
2 (3-inch) cinnamon sticks

2 whole cloves
1 tablespoon instant coffee powder
Milk or cream, if desired

Combine water, piloncillo or brown sugar, cinnamon sticks and cloves in a 2-quart measuring cup. Microwave on 100% (high) 5 minutes or until water begins to boil. Let stand 3 minutes; then stir. Strain mixture into another glass container, discarding cinnamon and cloves. Stir in coffee powder. Pour into cups or mugs. Serve with milk or cream, if desired.

Manzanas Asadas

Baked Apples

A perfect ending to any meal.

Power level: high
Cooking time: 8 to 10 minutes
Servings: 4

4 cooking apples
4 (3-inch) cinnamon sticks

1/3 cup packed brown sugar
2 tablespoons butter or margarine

Wash and core apples; place in an 8-inch-square baking dish. Insert a cinnamon stick into center of each apple. Press brown sugar around each cinnamon stick until hole is completely filled. Dot apples with butter or margarine; sprinkle with remaining brown sugar. Cover with waxed paper; microwave on 100% (high) 8 to 10 minutes, rotating dish after 4 minutes. Let stand 5 minutes. Apples should be tender. If more cooking is needed, cover with waxed paper; microwave on 100% (high) 1 minute or until tender. Remove cinnamon sticks. Serve apples hot.

Sopaipilla Mix

Although not made in a microwave, Sopaipillas are a wonderful addition to any meal.

Yield: 9-1/2 cups

8 cups all-purpose flour
2 tablespoons baking powder
2 teaspoons salt

1/4 cup sugar
1/2 cup vegetable shortening

Sift flour, baking powder, salt and sugar together in a bowl. Cut in shortening with a pastry blender or fork until mixture is the consistency of cornmeal. Place mixture in an airtight container. Store in a cool, dry place up to 3 months. Refrigerate for longer storage. Makes four recipes of Sopaipillas.

Sopaipillas

Fried Puffs

These delicate fried puffs go great with any meal or as a dessert.

Servings: 24

2-1/3 cups Sopaipilla Mix, page 152
2/3 cup warm water
1 cup vegetable shortening or vegetable oil

In a medium bowl, combine sopaipilla mix and warm water to make a medium dough. Turn out dough on a lightly floured board; knead lightly. Cover with a damp cloth; let stand 25 minutes. Roll out dough until about 1/8 inch thick. Cut into 3-inch squares.

Heat shortening or oil in a skillet or deep-fat fryer to 390F (200C) or until a 1-inch cube of bread turns golden brown in 20 seconds. Fat should be 1 to 2 inches deep. Deep-fry cut pieces of dough in hot fat. Hot fat will cause sopaipillas to puff. Turn sopaipillas in hot fat until both sides are golden brown. Remove and drain on paper towels to absorb excess fat. Sopaipillas can be filled with refried beans. As a dessert, fill with honey or roll in a mixture of ground cinnamon and sugar.

Like tortillas, sopaipillas are a favorite bread to go with main dishes or to be served as a dessert. Traditionally, they are fried in hot oil, however that is not a recommended practice in the microwave.

Caution: Do not attempt to deep-fat fry in your microwave oven. Still the best way to prepare sopaipillas is the traditional deep-fat frying in a skillet or deep-fat fryer.

Refresco de Melón

Melon Cooler

My great-grandmother prepared this melon cooler for church bazaars. Refresco de Melón is a seasonal drink. It will make any hot summer day refreshing. Serve over plenty of crushed ice.

Power level: high
Cooking time: 5 minutes
Servings: 6 to 8

1 medium cantaloupe
2 quarts water
1 cup sugar

1 cup diced watermelon
Mint sprigs or maraschino cherries,
**   if desired**

Remove seeds from cantaloupe; soak seeds in 2 quarts water overnight in the refrigerator. Cut cantaloupe flesh into small pieces; you will need 2 cups cantaloupe.

Strain cantaloupe seeds, reserving water and discarding seeds. In a glass bowl, combine 3 cups cantaloupe water and sugar. Microwave on 100% (high) 5 minutes or until sugar dissolves; cool slightly. Using a blender, process sweetened cantaloupe water with cantaloupe and watermelon pieces until pureed. Add mixture to remaining cantaloupe water; stir well. Serve cooler over crushed ice in goblets. Garnish each serving with a mint sprig or maraschino cherry, if desired.

Frozen treats can also be made. Pour this mixture into ice-cube trays. Insert a wooden stick into each cube. Freeze for delicious treats.

Variation

Honeydew can be substituted for cantaloupe, using the honeydew seeds as above.